The Essence of
Spiritual Awakening

The Essence of Spiritual Awakening

Enlightenment, Inspiration, and Insights that Illuminate the Path to Divinely Guided Wisdom

Judy White-Artz

Fresh Ink Group
Guntersville

The Essence of Spiritual Awakening

Enlightenment, Inspiration, and Insights that Illuminate the Path to Divinely Guided Wisdom

Copyright © 2023
by Judy White-Artz
All rights reserved

Fresh Ink Group
An Imprint of:
The Fresh Ink Group, LLC
1021 Blount Avenue #931
Guntersville, AL 35976
Email: info@FreshInkGroup.com
FreshInkGroup.com

Edition 1.0 2023

Cover design by Stephen Geez / FIG
Cover art by Anik / FIG
Book design by Amit Dey / FIG
Associate publisher Beem Weeks / FIG

Except as permitted under the U.S. Copyright Act of 1976 and except for brief quotations in critical reviews or articles, no portion of this book's content may be stored in any medium, transmitted in any form, used in whole or part, or sourced for derivative works such as videos, television, and motion pictures, without prior written permission from the publisher.

Cataloging-in-Publication Recommendations:
SEL004000 SELF-HELP / Affirmations
SEL016000 SELF-HELP / Personal Growth / Happiness
REL036000 RELIGION / Inspirational

Library of Congress Control Number: 2023920665

ISBN-13: 978-1-958922-56-9 Papercover
ISBN-13: 978-1-958922-57-6 Hardcover
ISBN-13: 978-1-958922-58-3 Ebooks

Dedication

I dedicate this book to my two beautiful granddaughters, Alexandra Jade and Brianna Caitlyn, whose bright light has graced my life with immense joy and love. I treasure the endless hours of "girl chat" we have shared laughing, talking, and reminiscing about all the experiences and memories we share and how all experiences in life lead us on a journey of discovering our true authentic self, as we evolve and embrace all of what life has to offer.

If I were to impart one gem of wisdom as guidance, it would be to remember that life flows like a river, bringing us new experiences and opportunities around every bend. Life is not defined by those moments in which we experience great sadness and disappointment. A new day will dawn and new opportunities for joy and happiness awaits us on the other side of those moments of challenge and crisis. All experiences in life serve a greater purpose to learn and grow in wisdom, strength, and courage along our path to enlightenment.

Let your light shine bright! I will always be with you to celebrate your milestones and accomplishments and encourage you in times of need.

I would like to give special recognition and gratitude to Sherry and Brian Rohr, Jan Sikes, and Deborah Allen. This book coming to fruition would not have been possible without the love, support, and encouragement of these loving souls.

My special connection to Sherry and Brian Rohr spans over twenty years. We have shared many life changing events together over the years, including their wedding, the birth of my granddaughters, the birth of their two children, and the passing of my husband, to name a few. There are no words to describe all the ways in which they have blessed my life or how much love I have for them. Without their abiding love and support, I would not have been able to fulfill my life purpose, which I believe includes the writing of this book. They are, and always will be, an integral part of my life and a cherished part of my heart.

My friend, Jan Sikes, was introduced to me by a mutual friend at the beginning stages of the creation of my book. Jan is the author of 17 books and her creative abilities continue to be revealed to me as our amazing friendship grows and evolves. I believe that God blesses us with special people in our lives that help guide us and enlighten us on our path to fulfill our purpose. Jan's knowledge, wisdom, and mentoring has been an integral part of the successful completion of this book and I am immeasurably blessed that she has graced my life.

My friendship with Deborah Allen blossomed over ten years ago. Deborah is an Accredited Life Coach and Tutor to young people, or adults, when the opportunity presents itself. Deborah is a very special soul and she has been such an amazing blessing in my life in so many ways. We, too, have shared many life changing events. Deborah and I share a passion for mentoring young people, giving them a voice, encouraging them, and helping them discover their unique and authentic self. Deborah has been my biggest cheerleader throughout the process of creating this book. She has generously given her time, energy, and support, without which the successful completion of this book would not have been possible.

I often marvel at all the amazing people that have graced my life and I am forever grateful for all the ways in which they have enriched my life.

Table of Contents

Dedication. v

Preface   Healing your Life with Divine Wisdom xi

Introduction. xiii

Prologue   Reflections of Life as a Child xv

Vignette 1   My Story Begins. 1

Vignette 2   An Epiphany, An Aha Moment 5

Vignette 3   The Power of the Mind 11

Vignette 4   An Experience in Enlightenment 17

Vignette 5   A Lesson in Inner Strength 21

Vignette 6   Trusting your Intuition; Death at my Door 25

Vignette 7   Perseverance; Sustaining Balance in Life 31

Vignette 8   Elements of a Healthy Relationship 37

Vignette 9   The Power of Words 45

Vignette 10   A Divine Blessing. 51

Vignette 11   An Extraordinary Life 59

Vignette 12   A Divine Gift. 67

Vignette 13   Messages of Love. 73

Vignette 14   Energy; The Gift of Life 83

Vignette 15   Reflections of Love. 89

Vignette 16   Garden of Inspiration 97

About Judy White-Artz 117

My Journal   Intentions, Gratitude, Thoughts, and Reflections. . . 119

PREFACE

Healing Your Life

Transforming your painful life experiences into steppingstones will move you forward on your life path by adding value, wisdom, and depth to your being. These experiences will then serve a meaningful purpose. We have the power to consciously shift our perception, which effectively shifts the pain of an experience into purpose. Now, we have something tangible to work with. Wisdom guides us not to focus our thoughts only on the negative aspects of an experience. Thoughts are powerful and what we seek, we will find. If we choose to focus all of our energy into the pain, we limit the possibility of expanding our perception and viewpoint to look at how this experience can bless our life and how we can "receive the lesson". The goal is to move forward in life, learn, and grow. Not to swirl around in a chaotic state of mind and stay stuck in that mindset. Use the value of your life experience to add wisdom and knowledge to become a more enlightened being. No one lives a life free from suffering. Sometimes, suffering comes from choices we have made and sometimes from choices our loved ones make that directly affect our life.

We all make mistakes. That is one of the ways we learn and grow. The hope is to "learn the lesson" it teaches us and not recreate the mistake. Learn, grow in wisdom, and move forward on our life path. Sometimes life events beyond our control occur, stemming from mother nature disasters, war, illnesses (such as the COVID pandemic), and these painful experiences affect millions of lives.

If we must suffer anguish and pain, I believe valuable life lessons will be learned and blessings will emerge as a result.

Introduction

My name is Judy. I was born in Southern California, which is an environment rich in people from many cultural backgrounds. Being raised in Southern California gave me the opportunity to meet and socialize with people from cultures all around the world.

I was raised in a middle-class home, so I didn't come from privileged, rich, or extraordinary means. This story reflects on some of the events that shaped my character, philosophies, and beliefs. I believe nothing in life happens by accident and all experiences add meaning and value to our life journey. If you are reading my story, perhaps you will find inspiration, a new perspective, or perhaps you can connect in a spiritual way to my story and recognize how many things happen in our daily life that shapes who we become. If I can touch one life or one heart with my story, it will add value and enrichment to my life and yours.

> *"Life isn't about where we live, what we are doing, and where we are going. The essence of life is "who we are", our authentic self. "Who we are" goes with us wherever we are, whatever we are doing".*
>
> **—Judy White-Artz**

Your unique being and gifts are a blessing from God and the Universe. What you do with these blessings and gifts is up to you.

The magic of life is in the journey of discovery. A gradual process of discovering our true authentic self. This process is a collection of our experiences, like pieces of a puzzle, that we piece together to form a unique work of art, years in the making.

PROLOGUE

Reflections of Life as A Child

Fill your senses with the beauty the world has to offer. It is not necessary to be financially abundant to live a life rich with blessings and experiences. Since I am now at the senior stage of my life, I find great joy in reflecting on how the experiences over my lifetime shaped my character and the values that I respect, honor, and live life by today. If I were asked what I am "most grateful for" in my years growing up as a young child, I would give great esteem to my family for teaching us how to find so much joy in small things. Teaching us how to use all our senses and "tune in" to the blessings and beauty that surround us every day. Beauty and joy are all around us, if we learn how to open our hearts and embrace the world using all our senses; sight, sound, taste, smell, and touch. Engaging our senses brings profound joy to our life. Our senses are a gift from God. Engaging our senses is a learned skill, as we are not born with this knowledge or appreciation. I am also eternally grateful that I was not taught prejudice, so I was free to find joy in learning how different cultures around the world live, the foods they cook, and the traditions they celebrate that warm their heart and honor their heritage.

At the time I grew up there were no electronic devices and we did not have a television until I was 10 years old. Telephones were on a "party line" system, so we shared a telephone line with other families. If you picked up the phone and someone else was on the line, you had to wait until they finished their conversation to use the phone. As dismal as that may sound by today's standards, in hindsight, I can see that this was a huge blessing to my life.

In my formative years, we were a family of modest means and didn't have a budget allotted for entertainment purposes. However, we never felt that we missed out of fun activities. We, instead, developed and used our creativity; there was no shortage of this element in our lives.

The joy of music was a part of our everyday life. Although we didn't have a television until my early teen years, we always had a radio. Music was such a joy in my home. We listened to all genres of music and everyone would sing-along. I always marveled at how beautifully my mother could sing harmony. Music and singing is always so joyful and uplifting. My grandparents had an old piano and both grandparents played the piano. When company visited, we would gather around the piano and sing together. As a young woman, my grandmother sang "on air" at a local radio station. Music was a huge part of our lives and remains so to this day.

My husband spoke seven languages and I discovered that there are two things in life that supercede language barriers and touch people's heart and soul, and is universal to all cultures; recognizing love and kindness and having an appreciation and joy of music. All people find joy in the expression of love, kindness, and the rhythm of music even if they speak a different language. Both gestures touch the heart and soul with no interpretation required.

In the 1950s when I was a young child, people had gardens and large front porches. People would go for a walk, sit on the porch to enjoy a chat with neighbors, swap stories and share a cup of coffee. We always felt a connection to our neighborhood and community. As a kid, we did simple things that were so much fun and no budget was required. We played hopscotch, jacks, marbles, and on hot days, we would run through the sprinklers while watering the lawn. Families played croquet in their front yards. Activities brought people together to share time with one another. We would go to the park, take a Sunday drive, and play a game in the car such as "I spy with my little eyes". We would look for any object that was a certain color, like all things blue; it could be a house, car, flower, sign, etcetera. The object was to see how many things we could find collectively. It was so much fun and taught us to be keenly observant of the world around us.

Sometimes, we would take a drive to nearby upscale areas. I remember so many charming and unique styles of homes, window shapes, different glass materials and designs; beveled glass, stained glass, frosted glass, etcetera. Have you ever noticed how beautiful dew drops on a plant, tree, or grass is? It looks like crystal when the sunlight shines upon it. Sometimes, we would drive to the beach to feel the cool salty air on our face, listen to and watch the waves crashing on the shore, and feel the sand beneath our feet. The sight and sound of water has always been very Zen to me; whether a babbling brook, river, ocean, waterfall, fountain, or the sound of rain.

As kids, we would make up our own games; like drawing a line with a piece of chalk, then draw a second line twenty feet back. We would all choose a rock or stone and see who could throw their stone and get closest to crossing the line but staying as close as possible to the line. We called it "Over the Line".

Most families planted a garden; some variety of fruits and vegetables. When it came time to harvest, there was usually more than one family could eat, so neighbors would share and swap. It was wonderful, not only did we reap the bounty of our garden, but we traded with other families, so we had an amazing variety of freshly grown produce. My grandparents had a large variety of fruit trees. The people that lived next door to my grandparent's house had chickens, so they would trade eggs for fresh fruit. What a fond memory and a nice wholesome way to live.

With all the amazing advances of new methods of conducting business and technology, there is still value to a more basic, simplified way of life. I consider myself very fortunate to have a full spectrum of exposure to the value of new advances in technology and still have an appreciation for savoring the style of life at an earlier time. I hold in my heart the joy and value of both experiences. I learned, however, that choosing to open your heart and awareness to the beauty of the world around you is a philosophy that brings profound joy to your life journey. This is timeless and is not dependent upon the timeline of your birth. This approach to living life, tuning into the world around you, and engaging all your senses is a timeless opportunity to embrace the joy of a more vibrant life; fully awakened to all the beauty the world has to offer. This philosophy can also be shared with others and become your legacy to your family. There is nothing more beautiful than the soul and energy of an awakened heart and mind.

You are blessed with the necessary tools. Will you choose to live life as a vibrant and enlightened human being? It is an important choice that rewards you with a life graced with blessings. On this chosen path, your energy becomes an inspiration and blessing to others. The question is, "Will you embrace the challenge?"

VIGNETTE 1

My Story Begins

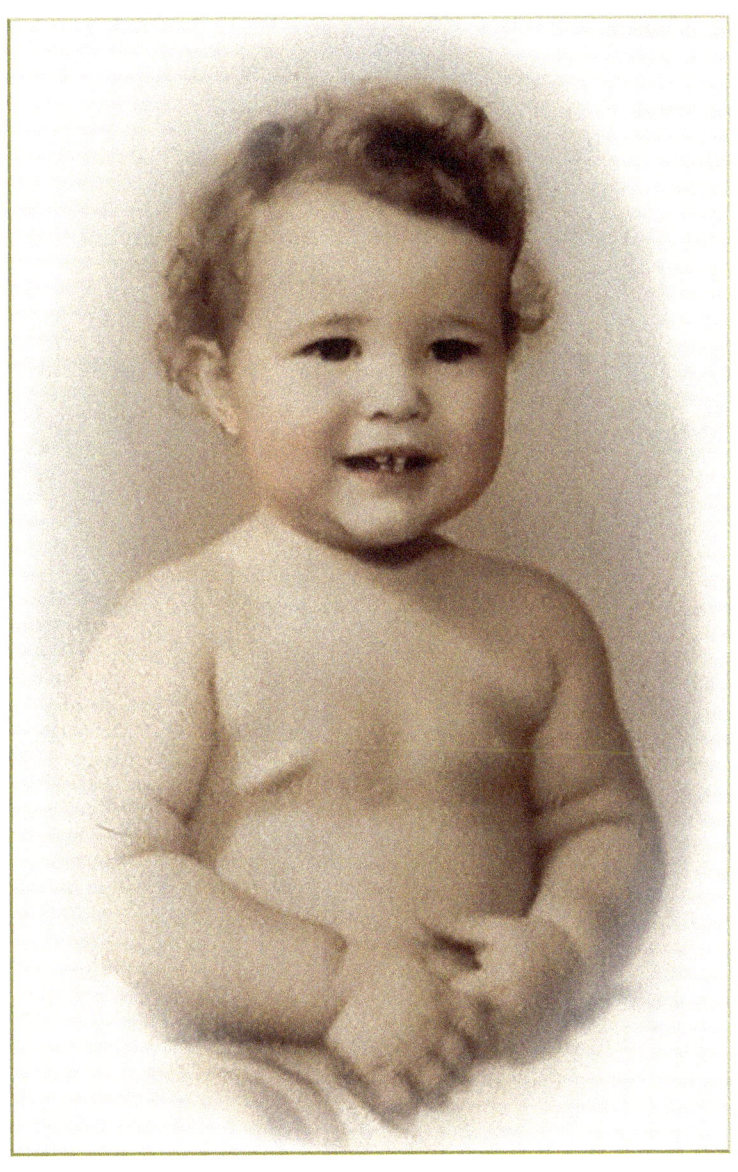

One of the earliest experiences I recall, as a young child, was when I started elementary school. My parents had separated and divorced before my sister and I started Kindergarten. In the early 1950s, the norm was for the father to work to support the family and the mother stayed at home to tend to the needs of the children and run the household by cooking, cleaning, laundry, ironing, etcetera. So, when I started school, kids would talk about their mom and dad and, naturally, would ask questions about my mom and dad. Since my mother was the primary parent, it was necessary for her to work to earn a living. It was difficult and awkward to have to try and explain where my dad was, why he didn't live with us, why my mother had to work, and why she couldn't be a stay-at-home mom.

So at the age of 5, with no life experience to speak of, here I am faced with an important choice. Do I share a story that my new friends will understand and relate to, or do I say the truth with all the courage

I can muster and risk being marked as "different" from the norm and subject myself to negative reaction, commentary, and feedback.

I learned at a very young age the value of standing in my truth. When we tell an untruth, or lie, we create a web of deceit that perpetuates more lies to sustain the lie and not expose it. So, I chose to state my truth which was painful for me and took a lot of courage.

To be clear, my mother was a wonderful, warm, and compassionate human being, so I was not deprived of a loving home to grow up in. My dad was a veteran, he served in the Navy. He was a talented musician. He played the piano, keyboard, and guitar. My favorite memory was when he would sit down at the piano and play Boogie Woogie, it was amazingly joyful. Although my dad was not a major part of my daily life, my sister and I did see him on a regular basis. The truth is, I always felt that, with my dad, our roles were reversed. My dad had developed a drinking problem and, although he was not abusive to us, when he was drinking, he was loud and boisterous, which was offensive and embarrassing to me. As a result, he left me feeling like he was the needy one in our relationship; not the mentor that I could turn to for insight, strength, and guidance. My sister and I also had wonderful grandparents on my mother's side, that lived nearby, with which we shared a lot of love and quality time. My grandmother was a nurse and my grandfather was a firefighter.

The jewel of wisdom to be gained from this experience is that we are always making choices in life. Standing in our truth takes courage, but is so freeing and rewarding over the course of our life. When we are our true, authentic self, we attract people that are genuinely drawn to our energy and essence for the right reasons and not because we are playing a role; trying to fit into the "norm" of who we think would be more likeable, which is a deception to ourselves and others. All through life, we have moments where we can choose to take the high road, and remain true to ourselves, or not speak our truth, which takes us on a long journey to lie after lie to sustain the false image we chose to create.

Taking the high road is far more courageous and rewarding, but also, in the process of developing courage and being brave, leads to personal growth and adds to our sense of pride, accomplishment, and enlightenment.

VIGNETTE 2

An Epiphany, An Aha Moment

Sometimes in life, we discover that we have knowledge or wisdom and we don't know where this wisdom came from.

As a child, I was interested in the diversity of the religions around the world. My mother bought me a book on this subject. I instinctively knew that all religions had value and purpose; to believe in something and someone greater than ourselves. Love always prevails over fear and evil. Truth always comes to the light.

As a young girl, I knew intrinsically that all religions had great value. I was not taught this, but I knew that whatever religion we are drawn to, for inspiration and motivation, will help us to stay on our life path to be a kind and loving person, make good choices, and radiate positive, loving energy into the Universe. Whatever your chosen religion is, the purpose is universal; to guide and inspire us to make good choices in life. If we make a choice that doesn't lead to a place of peace and harmony, we can draw strength from our religious beliefs and redirect our focus and energy to get back on track.

Our life journey is about learning to love and loving to learn. Since we can't teach without learning, we come full circle and benefit from the experience of others, as well as our own.

I would like to share a prayer that I wrote with you in celebration of life, honoring all of the cultures that inhabit our world.

A Prayer: Celebration of Life

Life is precious,
Life is fragile.
Life is "strong".
Fill my senses with the music of life, each instrument creating part of a symphony; an orchestra of joy, depth, and spirituality.

Let me enjoy the beauty of God's creations that surround me, nature in all its glory.

Let me be open to the expansiveness of the world's many cultures, traditions, and religions that comprise our planet.

Let me honor and respect that there is a place for differences, as well as comfort in that with which we are familiar.

Let me recognize "all" that God has created is sacred and that our life lessons and experiences can also help others; we can use our pain and suffering to create understanding, knowledge, and wisdom.

I believe that if we must suffer pain and anguish, there is a way to make these lessons serve a higher purpose by creating understanding and wisdom, which adds value to our life.

Is it not our purpose in life to learn to love and love to learn? To honor life's many teachers and lessons?

The challenge in life is to find ways to honor the spirit of God and the Universe. To celebrate our diversity, as well as honoring those who share our beliefs and values.

Human dignity, love, and respect must prevail in a civilized world; only then can we feel the love and light of a peaceful world – in our neighborhood, in our community, at our churches, in our state, and in our nation.

Make your legacy to your children and your family be a legacy of love.

Rise above hate.

Rise above anger.

Come from your heart with love. Use your God given energy and light to do "good" in this world.

Be a light in the darkness. A ray of hope.

We can heal; As an individual, a family, a community, a nation.

"You" have the power to make a difference in this world.

Make this Universe a better place; A place where love prevails over hate, good prevails over evil, light prevails over darkness, and wisdom prevails over ignorance.

We are all God's children.

Let us come together for the greater good of all people.

Let your light shine bright; "Illuminate the truth".

Don't add to what is wrong with this world, be a radiant example of a loving human being.

Turn your heart light on. Give love and reflect God's light to others.

<u>You</u> are our hope for a better world.

Embrace the Challenge!!

VIGNETTE 3

The Power of our Mind

In my mid twenties, I attended a motivational seminar in which the speaker presented an inspirational example of the power of our thoughts and mind that resonated with me throughout my life and is still impactful to my life today. A powerful and timeless lesson and visual image of the power of our mind.

The speaker said, "Imagine if I placed a plank of wood on the floor which is a foot wide and 20 feet long and I asked you to walk across this plank from one side to the other." You would not hesitate to accept this challenge.

Now, imagine if I raised and elevated this same plank of wood 2 feet off the ground. You may hesitate, but would probably accept the challenge to walk across the plank. Now, you have allowed your mind to introduce a degree of doubt and fear that there is some danger of falling off the plank of wood, even though you know you walked across this same plank successfully with no danger at ground level.

Now, imagine that this same plank of wood was elevated 20 feet above the ground. Your focus now shifts to the danger and fear of falling off the plank, instead of having confidence in safely walking from one side of the plank to the other. Your fear would probably prevail and lead you to make the decision to "not" take this risk, even though you have successfully walked across this same plank in the previous two scenarios.

This is one amazing example of how we allow fear to limit the choices we make in life. In reality, no one limits us in life. We limit ourselves. You have to ask yourself, how much power do I want to give to fear? We have the power to shift our thoughts to positive belief in our ability to have new experiences in life without negative consequences. It is up to us to empower ourselves with positive thoughts and choices that lead to new experiences and adventures as we move through our life journey.

This experience was confirmation to me that there are two basic emotional elements in life, love or fear. All choices either come from love or fear and we hold the power over our thoughts.

Remember that everything we do in life starts with a single thought. A very powerful revelation and concept. Fear limits us, love empowers us. Of course, we need to give careful consideration and thought into the choices we make to assure that they add value to our life, and those we love, and that these choices contribute to our greater good and higher self.

Think of Life as a Wishing Well

Sometimes, we think of life as a wishing well.

If we pour out our thoughts, dreams, and desires, that they will blossom, come to fruition, and return to us in the form of happiness and fulfillment.

In reality, life is a journey. We choose our path and the only thing we really have control over is how we respond to the challenges that befall us along the way.

No one is an exception to these opportunities to learn, grow, and develop wisdom and grace in the face of anguish and pain.

If we choose a path that does not bring us to a place of peace and harmony, there is always a new opportunity to redirect our choices that will lead us to a better place, a place of grace with love, harmony, and joy at the center of our thoughts and actions.

This path comes with the responsibility to show compassion and love to others that cross our path and leads to enlightenment and a deeper joy for the essence of life and its many lessons and teachers.

VIGNETTE 4

An Experience in Enlightenment

In my late twenties, a lady I worked with charted my astrological chart and the position of the planets at the exact moment of my birth.

The overall message was illuminating and clear. She said it was revealed over and over in my chart that my destiny was to be a teacher. She stated that she was amazed and had never seen such a strong message repeated in an astrological chart; Teacher, teacher, teacher.

At this point in my life, I thought about how I had planned to go to college to become an elementary school teacher, but had been lead to follow the path of becoming an Administrative Assistant because I had a skill set that made me successful in that endeavor. For a long time, I wondered if I had made a major mistake in choosing my career path. Had I not followed the path that God intended for me to use my unique gifts? Life is a journey of discovering truth. Truth about ourselves, our ideals, beliefs, and relationships. All good and loving things worthy of our energy, devotion, and commitment must come from truth.

If we discover that a belief, or relationship, is not based on truth, we must use this revelation to reevaluate our truth and what we stand for. If an ideal or relationship reveals it is no longer worthy of our trust and respect because it is not based on truth, it is no longer worthy of our energy.

An ideal, belief, or relationship must be based on truth and respect to add value to our life.

I believe the purpose of life is to love and be loving. I believe that nothing in life has more purpose than our connection to others. Love heals. We mustn't let our light be dimmed. "Be the light" in time of darkness. Choose vulnerability over fear, love over hate, empathy over judgment. Putting energy into loving ourselves and others helps us to heal life's traumas.

Illuminate the truth.
Choose wisely.
Stand in your truth.
Be a light.

VIGNETTE 5

A Lesson of Inner Strength

When I was twenty-eight years old the world as I knew it completely fell apart. My beloved mother passed away unexpectedly from leukemia at the young age of forty-eight years old. My world collapsed all around me. The pain and anguish of her loss was so unbearable, I wasn't certain I would be able to work through the grief and heal.

My mother was a major part of my life. I spoke with her on a daily basis. She had been having symptoms of the flu, so I told her I would pick her up and take her to the doctor for a checkup. When I arrived to pick up my mother, it was abundantly clear to me that she was so sick, she would not have been capable of driving herself.

A blood test revealed that she had acute (advanced) leukemia. The doctor had me transport her directly to the hospital. Lab test results indicated the advanced progression of her disease. She was admitted to the hospital on Thursday and passed on Sunday. Prior to her doctor visit, no one had a clue that her life journey was coming to an end.

In this period of this overwhelming disbelief came the responsibility of sharing with loved ones what had happened. We had to reveal to my Grandmother that her only child had passed. The hysteria of this news rippled over and over as family and friends tried to absorb the loss of my mother's life at such a young age.

It was incomprehensible and everyone felt that her life was cut short and was somehow incomplete. The energy and sadness of her loss was so incredibly heavy to bear.

At twenty-eight years old, the only previous experience I had with the death of a loved one was when my beloved Grandfather passed from a heart attack when I was sixteen and he was seventy-three years old. In the passing of my Grandfather, I felt that he had lived a full life and it was his time to be called home. I grieved his loss and the loss of him leaving my physical world, but I felt comforted that he had fulfilled what he came here to do.

With my Mother's passing, it felt like she had been cheated out of a full life journey.

For the next couple of years, I felt like I was walking around with a huge, dark cloud over my head and I was perpetually surrounded by tremendous sadness and grief.

I was very young and inexperienced with the pain of losing a loved one so much a part of my heart. My son was eight years old when my Mother passed, so I knew I had to continue to participate in life and keep going for the sake of my loved ones still living. That is what my Mother would want me to do. Keep my heart light glowing and reflect love to my family. So, I used that thought as inspiration and drew upon my inner strength to help me move forward with and through the pain.

Much to my surprise, I did have this inner strength to call upon. Sometimes we find inspiration in the most unexpected places. There was a charming shop in Redondo Beach, California that specialized in selling international coffee and tea. I stopped there to pick up specialty coffee for a gift. It was such a divine aromatherapy experience. The aroma of freshly brewed coffee and tea was heavenly. Much to my surprise, I discovered many other charming products in that store. To my amazement, there was a book rack that drew my interest. I picked up a book by Raymond Moody called "Life After Life". I thought it looked like a fascinating subject, so I purchased it.

As I look back, I feel I was divinely guided to go to that shop that day and connect with this amazing book, which turned out to be a steppingstone to enlightenment about what happens when we die and our purpose in life.

The book is based on a study that Dr. Raymond Moody conducted regarding near-death events that people had experienced and the common thread of these experiences. The subjects were all ages, from many different geographical locations, and the reason for their near-death experience was wide-ranging.

This book turned out to be pivotal and enlightening to me not only about the process of death itself, but about our life purpose. Once again, a message and confirmation to me emphasizing the importance of the choices we make on our life journey. Most of us do not have a second chance at life, so we must learn that how we live our life really does matter. So, don't take it lightly and rise to the challenge.

Remember, love is not hurtful, painful, or a struggle. Genuine love brings comfort, joy, and inspiration to our life and inspires us to aspire to achieve a higher level of consciousness and connect to our higher self.

VIGNETTE 6

Trusting Your Intuition; Death at My Door

Around the age of thirty years old, I had a very rude awakening. I suddenly experienced excruciating pain on my right side, at waist level. I had stopped by my sister-in-law's house to pick up my son, but I was in so much pain that I, quite literally, could not get out of the car. My husband picked me up and took me to the emergency room at the nearest hospital. They did an x-ray but could not identify the problem. They released me and advised me to see my doctor the next day. The next day, when my doctor examined me, he determined immediately that my gallbladder was dangerously swollen and advised us to go directly to the hospital and that he would be right behind us. My doctor was fearful that my gallbladder would burst. When he ran tests, he couldn't see any gallstones or a granular problem to cause the swollen gallbladder, but stated we must do an exploratory surgery immediately, as my gallbladder was in danger of bursting, which would be life threatening. I thought that perhaps I could wait to see if I would feel better, but my doctor stated this was not an option. He walked me upstairs and we prepared for surgery. Because it wasn't a surgery we planned for in advance, the doctors gave me just enough anesthetic to get me through the surgery. So, I actually regained consciousness while still in the operating room. That was extremely frightening to me, but fortunately the surgery was completed. The doctor advised me that I shocked them all when they discovered that I had a perforated ulcer. All that toxic poison was dumping onto my gallbladder and into my body. I was told if we had waited any longer, I could have died from blood poisoning, peritonitis. They surgically cleaned, sutured, and repaired the ulcer. The healing was now up to me.

After the initial shock of understanding that I could have died, had the doctor not insisted on the exploratory surgery, I had to reflect on what caused me to get to this dangerous point, as my life was in jeopardy and one thing was crystal clear, I certainly wanted to participate in my life, not contribute to my death.

After an abundance of deep thought and reflection, I learned everything I could about what "not" to do to sustain good health. I recognized that I hadn't been feeling well for a very long time. I was not eating properly and I was going long periods of time between meals. This habit allowed my stomach acid to eat at the lining of my empty stomach. I was also taking aspirin daily because I wasn't feeling well which, in essence, is like pouring acid on an already irritated stomach lining.

I started to formulate a plan to heal my struggling body. First, I started to eat breakfast in the morning because the stomach goes the longest period of time between dinner and overnight until breakfast. I stopped taking aspirin, which is purely acidic. I took an antacid during the healing process and eliminated spices and spicy foods so that my body would be fully able to heal itself. I put all of my energy into healing myself using my mind, body, and spirit. I did everything in moderation and made time for proper rest, which is also essential for healing. Six to eight weeks later, I circled back for x-rays to check the healing status of my ulcer. After the x-rays, the radiology doctor very pompously asked me, "What makes you think you have an ulcer?" I was taken aback by his sarcastic remark, but advised the doctor of my emergency surgery for a perforated ulcer six to eight weeks prior. The Radiologist advised there was "no" evidence of an ulcer. I was thrilled and relieved and was determined never to recreate this life-threatening event ever again.

Now that I brought about the physical healing of my body, I was ready to go deeper into the thoughts and feelings that I had been ignoring and hadn't been honoring. I gave careful consideration and thought to how I really felt about my life. I loved my husband, but after twenty years, we were no longer moving in the same direction. Our priorities and goals had somehow shifted and we were drifting apart. I had these thoughts and feelings before, but I thought it was not nice or fair for me to have these feelings and, therefore, did not honor my thoughts and feelings. When we do not honor our true authentic self, it not only isn't true to ourself, but the other people in our life that we love and care about. We must illuminate and accept the truth and make life choices based on that truth.

Over time, it became abundantly clear that my husband and I were no longer in sync about what was important to us and, as a couple, we were pursuing a different path. We were pulling in different directions and the healthiest choice was to end the marriage, so we could remain true to our authentic self and be free to put energy into choices that would bring us both joy and happiness. It is always painful to make this kind of life decision, but sometimes it is healthier to move forward in life and not hang onto a relationship that is no longer based on common ground and shared goals. Sometimes, we need to love someone enough to honor that they are also a unique being on a life journey, as we are, and we must choose not to cling to a relationship for the wrong reasons, such as our fear for the future. A future that will lead us both to new life experiences and lessons and allow us to grow in wisdom. We must allow love to set us free and follow our own path to enlightenment and the discovery of our unique life purpose.

> **We betray our true selves when we do not follow our hearts desire, for what the heart is attracted to is your destiny.**
>
> **—Leon Brown**

Every connection and relationship that we experience in life has purpose and adds value to our life journey. Even when relationships change and we move in a new direction, they serve the purpose of helping us learn and grow in wisdom on our journey to discover our true authentic self. Hold the joyous memories in your heart and recognize that life is constant and flowing, like a river, leading us to new experiences. Sometimes along our journey, we experience rough waters (challenges) and sometimes it is smooth sailing. Rejoice in both, as we would not know true joy, if we didn't encounter challenges to test our courage, strength, and our ability to survive the rough waters.

The valuable lesson this experience taught me is to trust and honor our thoughts and feelings and stay true to our authentic self. My higher self (intuition) was giving me a message, but I chose to ignore those feelings by pushing them away because I believed it wasn't fair for me to put energy into thoughts and feelings that may be hurtful to others. My higher self, however, knew my truth and even though I wasn't addressing these feelings externally, it was eating away at me internally, and taking a dangerous toll on my health and well-being. I almost paid the ultimate price of losing my life. If your intuition is sending you strong thoughts and feelings about a situation in your life, you must respect the message and honor your true feelings. Just because we choose not to deal with a situation, that does not mean it doesn't affect our health and well-being, as it can continue to eat away at us and ultimately cause our bodies to become sick. Remember, thoughts are powerful and the power of our thoughts and beliefs is in our hands. Honor yourself and stand in your truth.

VIGNETTE 7

Perseverance; Sustaining Balance in Life

Have you ever experienced a series of circumstances or events that came together and caused the "perfect storm" that created an event that abruptly turned your life upside down? A tower moment that you had no choice but to address? That moment in my life is what I want to share with you in this experience.

I was around forty years old and divorced. My son had graduated from high school, was working full-time, and was still at home. My mother had passed away and my grandmother moved in with me after her quadruple heart bypass surgery. I had a huge responsibility and was determined to assure everyone in my household was well taken care of. My focus was intent on being successful in my job and assuring that, as our primary source of income, I was able to take good care of the three of us.

I was focusing all my energy into being successful at my job and keeping my house in order feeling, no matter what, that was imperative and needed to be given my primary focus. Nothing else was more important than that goal. No matter what, I had to keep going. I realize now that I had tunnel vision.

I didn't feel well, but I went to work anyway. At work, I suddenly felt faint and got extremely weak. I realized that, over a long period of time, I had been losing a lot of blood through my menstrual cycle and had even been experiencing more than one period a month. I thought this change was taking place due to my age and that it was probably my new normal. How wrong I was. Later the doctor advised me that, over time, I had actually been hemorrhaging.

I became so sick at work that my boss arranged for my coworker and friend to take me to the doctor, as he determined it was unsafe for me to drive. We called my Gynecologist and he worked me into his schedule. When I got to his office, I had a fever of 104 degrees, which is dangerous for an adult. He immediately sent me to the hospital to be admitted for tests to diagnose the basis of my health problem.

Diagnostic tests revealed that I had a bowel infection and a blood test revealed my hemoglobin level was half of what it should be. I was severely anemic, which left my body with no ability to fight off infection, an extremely dangerous situation for my health and well-being.

My doctor explained that severe anemia interferes with levels of oxygen circulating throughout the body and I could easily faint without proper oxygen. He ordered me not to get out of bed without a nurse present. My Gynecologist immediately called in other specialists; an Internist to tend to the bowel infection and a Hematologist to address the hemoglobin issue. The end goal was to restore my health so that we could schedule a hysterectomy, which was the root cause of the blood loss and was endangering my health. All of these issues were of grave concern and could be life-threatening if not resolved.

I was initially in the hospital for two weeks. The internist told me that, under normal circumstances, I would have come to his office and been prescribed an antibiotic, which would have healed the infection but, due to the hemoglobin issue, my body was struggling to fight and heal the infection.

It was necessary for him to prescribe an extremely strong antibiotic to heal the infection, but that also killed the good bacteria, along with the bad, so I ended up getting Dysentery, historically prevalent in World War I, causing many deaths. As it turned out, I was allergic to the two medications normally prescribed to heal Dysentery, so I had to be given a thick serum by injection into my already painfully bruised hips.

Once again, there was no choice, as my survival was at risk. At that time, the Hematologist had prescribed injections of Vitamin B and other medications to build up my blood to normal levels so we could schedule the hysterectomy surgery, which was the root problem and causing the blood loss due to Endometriosis, a disease of the uterus.

At one point, all three Specialists were standing over me in my hospital bed (my Gynecologist, Internist, and Hematologist) discussing their concern over the fact that my blood count was not improving as quickly as they expected and they were contemplating the need to schedule a blood marrow test (thinking strongly about the possibility that I may have Leukemia).

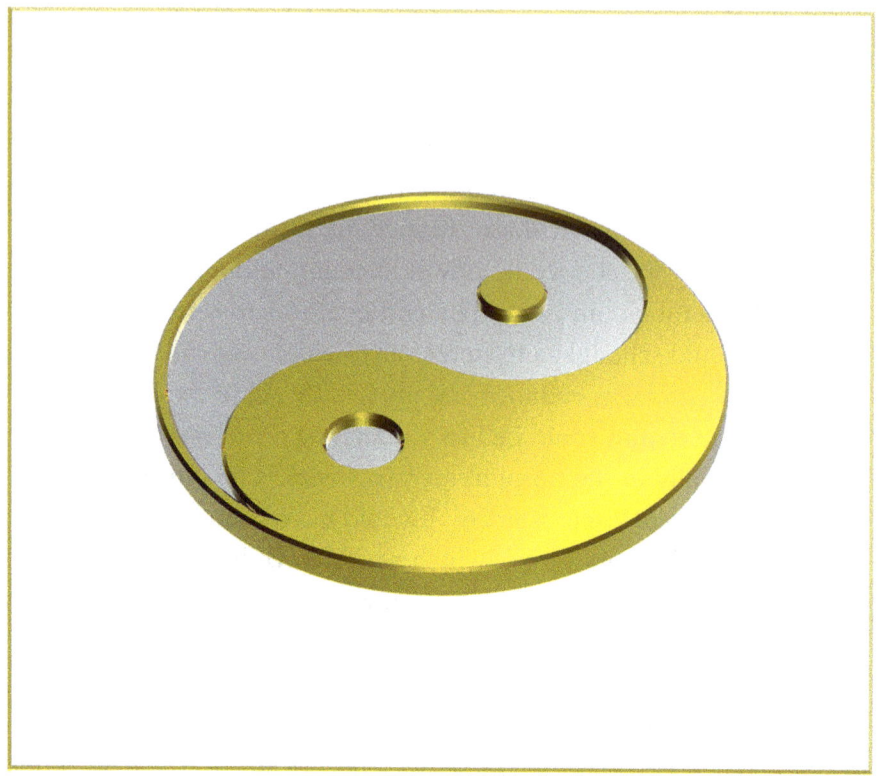

At that moment, I had an epiphany, I knew that it wasn't my time to leave this earth. I startled all of them by proclaiming it was not my time to leave this earth, and we should wait before deciding a bone marrow test was necessary. For a moment, it was completely silent, as they were all shocked. Then, they reluctantly decided to give my body a bit more time to regenerate and improve.

Shortly thereafter, my blood tests started to show slow improvement. I was released from the hospital to continue to rebuild my blood levels at home in preparation for the hysterectomy.

During this time, I realized that although work is an important element in our life, it pales in comparison to our health and well-being. First and foremost, we must tune-in to our bodies and not disregard symptoms which need to be discussed with a medical professional. If we do not take care of ourselves, we cannot use the gifts God has given us to experience life and fulfill our life purpose. I was committed and determined to do "whatever was necessary" to restore my health and put renewed energy into living life. I vowed to heal myself.

Approximately one month after my original hospitalization, we were able to schedule my hysterectomy. I was off work for a total of two and half months. My experience was horrific, but I was so blessed to have doctors that were wonderful human beings, as well as good doctors.

My Gynecologist faithfully checked on me whenever he was at the hospital, as he was so concerned over how ill I was. Even in crisis, there are always blessings that surround us.

The valuable life lesson I learned from this experience is to tune-in to your body. Discuss any changes or symptoms you are experiencing with a medical professional. Life is strong, but life can also be fragile. Do not narrow your focus and attention on only one area of your life. Maintain a balance to sustain a healthy and rewarding life. Good health is imperative in order to experience all the joy life has to offer. Nothing is more important than participating in good health; mind, body and spirit. **Gem of Wisdom:** Choosing to ignore an issue does not mean it doesn't exist.

VIGNETTE 8

Elements of A Healthy Relationship

The essence of life is deeply rooted in our connection to others. Through our friendships, relationships, and experiences with other people, we learn about life, evolve and grow in wisdom, learn about ourselves, and form our unique philosophies and beliefs. I believe in the basic good of all people. However, as we all have different experiences and challenges in life at different times, our needs ebb and flow and we aren't always able to make a meaningful connection with everyone along our path. I strongly believe that every experience has value. Negative or painful experiences can define what we don't want in our life, therefore, are also a valuable lesson. Wisdom that Maya Angelou once shared, (not an exact quote) "People may not remember what you said or what you did, but they will always remember how you made them feel."

We should all treat others as we would like to be treated, with kindness, trust, mutual respect, and a caring heart. As human beings, we all have times we struggle with difficult challenges that life presents us with. It is at these times that I am most grateful for my enduring friendships. Friends that will stand by your side and help you through whatever you are struggling with. A good friend will listen carefully and share their wisdom with truth and honesty, to help you gain clarity, so you can move forward with courage and strength. They remind you that you are not alone. Good friends are a blessing from God. God provides us with friends and earthly angels to help us on our journey.

> *"Friends lift us up when our wings forget how to fly."*
> **Author Unknown**

Valued friendships that bless our life have the qualities of love, kindness, mutual trust, respect, and honesty. If you lose trust, respect, and honesty in a relationship, you must think carefully if it is worthy of your energy moving forward, as the element of trust, honesty, and respect are the building blocks necessary for a meaningful relationship. Without these qualities, you must ask yourself, what value is this relationship bringing into your life?

Sometimes, friendships start out in a positive way, but surprisingly shift in an unexpected way. I would like to share a couple of experiences I have had that taught me how to identify unhealthy patterns in a relationship that ultimately caught me completely off guard and left me totally bewildered, shocked, and surprised by the reality of the true nature of the other person.

A co-worker who slowly became a friend seemed relaxed, funny, and engaging. As I got to know them, they were fun and seemed kind and caring. What anyone would look for in a friendship. At the time, I was struggling in my marriage and was contemplating what changes might be necessary in my life, which I now see left me very vulnerable and not in my usual solid, strong state of mind.

I was enjoying my new friendship until, over time, I noticed that this person was constantly creating drama and chaos and I was miserable. They would get upset at something I would say or do, or I would not say or do something they thought I should have. They would be angry, dump their anger on me, and then were not available to talk it out; referred to as ghosting. I was scrambling to keep things on an even keel, keep them happy, and it was taking all of my energy. I slowly realized they were manipulating my feelings and I was in a "no win" situation. I was miserable and I could clearly see that no amount of effort on my part was ever going to change the situation. After much careful and conscientious thought, I suddenly realized that "everything" was about them, they took no responsibility for their behavior and they were a master at manipulating the facts to shift all the responsibility to me for whatever they were upset and unhappy about. So, unless I wanted to continue to be this person's "puppet", I needed to stop putting energy into a friendship designed to fill the needs of one person, who always had to be the center of attention, constantly created drama and chaos, never accepted responsibility for their behavior, and was completely self-absorbed. There was no consideration being given to my thoughts and feelings. The truth was evident that this friendship was not mutually rewarding. Since I am committed to putting energy into mutually rewarding relationships, I chose not to spend one more minute of my life as someone's puppet. As I said earlier, negative experiences can teach us what we don't want in our life; lesson learned.

Sometimes in life, someone really close to our heart, in our inner circle, chooses a life partner or spouse that exhibits some of these unhealthy personality traits, as previously noted in this article, that sets off a chain of events that completely changes your life by default. Not because of any choice you have made, but the effect is no less painful. I wanted to note my personal experience with this type of scenario with compassion for those who have suffered through this type of experience.

I fully believe that everyone should make choices that will bring them great joy and fulfill their life with the deep love we all are seeking. I believe that, most of the time, our relationships can thrive and flourish and we can find a way of blending new, important relationships with existing relationships with friends and family. Sadly, this is not always the case.

All healthy relationships require the devotion of time and loving energy from <u>both</u> parties to be mutually rewarding and sustain a loving connection.

In my later years, I have learned a great deal about the characteristics of the narcissist personality. This concept was relatively new to me, so I did a lot of research to learn more about the elements of a narcissistic personality, as I recognized a correlation to my previous experiences. I, subsequently, have also heard other people's recollections of their personal experiences with individuals with these same characteristics.

I would like to point out that when we are critiquing the value of a friendship or relationship, it is the overall history that is of value; how we interact overall. At times, we will all disappoint someone along our journey; sometimes we are the strength for others and sometimes we are in need of that strength. As human beings, we all have a different way of perceiving a situation; we may have to agree to disagree. It is our "intention" that is most important. If we do not intend to do harm, or be hurtful, our intention will be judged before our action and choices.

Once you have had an experience with a narcissistic personality and learn the characteristics, you can more easily spot the signs and hopefully avoid reliving the nightmare and be able to shift your energy, time, and attention to healthier relationships.

I would like to point out some of the personality traits of a narcissist so you can be aware of what to recognize as potential red flags. Please understand that we all, at times, may exhibit some of these behaviors, but if someone has a combination of these behaviors consistently, you may wish to give careful thought and consideration to your relationship with this person.

Traits of a Narcissistic Personality:

1. Always must be the center of attention; excessively talk about themselves.
2. Grandiose ideas, unrealistic; indulge in fantasy.
3. Egotistical sense of superiority.
4. Entitlement; Do not take responsibility for their behavior.
5. Must always be the one "in control".

6. Lack of empathy.
7. Lack of boundaries.
8. Indulge themselves; Rant and rave, bully behavior.
9. Manipulative behavior; Will do "whatever is necessary" to appear in the right, including deceiving others and lying.

I have observed through my experiences that the narcissist says things like, "If you did not say this or do that, I would not have behaved the way that I did." Again, they accept no responsibility for anything they say or their behavior.

In speaking with others about their experiences with the narcissist personality and reflecting on my own experiences, I see one common thread that I would like to share; the narcissist typically chooses people who are at a vulnerable time in life, struggling, not in a strong state of mind and they are, therefore, more easily manipulated. In the beginning, the narcissist is usually charming, funny, and showers you with attention. They "suck you in" and, over time, they eliminate competing friendships and family relationships and you slowly become their puppet. Your life revolves solely around them. The narcissist decides who to socialize with, what activities you will do together, etcetera. They make all the decisions in the relationship and household. Ultimately, it is your choice if this is a fulfilling way to live your life.

When people behave cruelly, they come up with a multitude of excuses to justify their behavior. Sometimes, they even convince themselves you were deserving of their treatment. The reality is that being cruel is never acceptable.

Gems of Wisdom

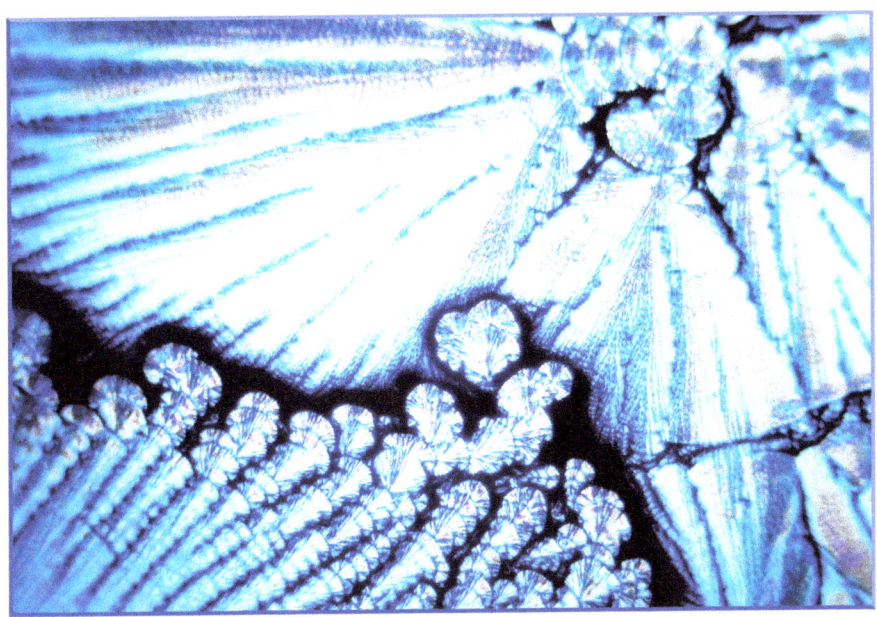

This is on You:

- *Your Behavior*
- *The choices you make*
- *The way you live*
- *The way you think*

Remember, your perception creates and manifests your reality.

"How people treat you is their karma; how you react is your karma".

Buddhist Quote

You cannot change where you come from, but you can change where you are going. A parting thought; rejection is projection. You are not rejected; you are just redirected. Our worst experience can turn into our greatest blessing. Keep moving forward; new experiences await you.

Mantra

Today, I choose happiness.
I have faith in my journey.
Every experience is helping me grow and evolve into someone I can be proud of.
Every day is a new beginning.
I will stop thinking about what could have been or what should have been said or done.
When I choose to see the good in others, I will illuminate the good in myself.
I will be <u>Strong</u> enough to let go of what does not serve me,
<u>Wise</u> enough to move forward.
<u>Honest</u> enough to work hard,
<u>Patient</u> enough to wait for the blessings I have earned along the way.

Gem of Wisdom

Light a candle in the darkness – Illuminate the truth.
Participate in life – You can heal.
One step at a time, replace fear with love for yourself and others.
Love heals.

—**Judy White-Artz**

VIGNETTE 9

The Power of Words

Your thoughts and Words Shape your World

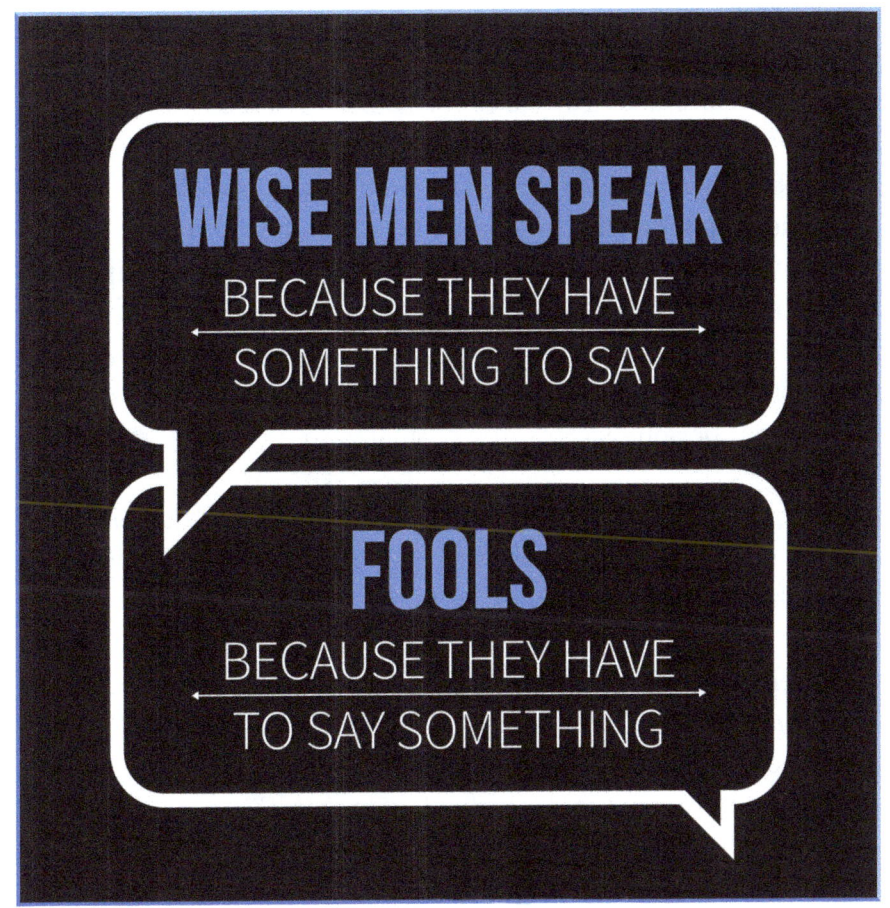

This segment is about the art of communication and the power of words. Communication is the verbal and written expression of our thoughts, feelings, ideas, and intentions. There is a huge difference between speaking "with" someone and speaking "at them".

I have a story to share with you which is a cherished memory for me. My two granddaughters, Alexandra and Brianna, were having a sleepover at my house. They were about 10 years old at the time (they are fraternal twins). We always find great joy in our "girl chats". We talk endlessly about every subject you can imagine. We observed an unpleasant conversation between people we didn't know. The subject came up about how people talk to each other.

I shared with them how powerful words are. Once you say something, you can't take it back. So, it is best to choose wisely. "Think first" before you speak and give thought to what you want your message to be. If you act in an irrational manner, the focus will be on your "behavior" and not your message. The goal is to deliver your message in a way that it can be received and considered without shifting the attention to your behavior.

The essence of successful communication lies in thought and presentation. The true power of words is to deliver a meaningful message.

A wise person accepts responsibility to deliver a meaningful message,

A fool believes they are entitled to speak without the wisdom of forethought, leaving no doubt their message is probably self-serving and lacks in value.

The true value and power of communication is in the exchange of intelligent thoughts, beliefs, and ideas.

I shared with my granddaughters that, "If you are the recipient of someone's mean and hurtful words, all you can do is remember how that feels and vow not to do that with your words".

Suddenly, Brianna looked up at me and said, "Grammie, you sound like Gandhi." An amazing "aha" moment. It was crystal clear to me that they both understood the philosophy of my message. They are so bright, at ten years old they knew who Gandhi was and were aware of his brilliant philosophies. I had no idea that they had this knowledge. Such wisdom for children at such a young age. From that moment on, they started calling me "Grammie Gandhi" because of my love for planting seeds of wisdom.

The value of the art of communication in our lives, verbal and written, is priceless, as it affects every aspect of our life; our education, career, marriage, personal relationships, business, etcetera. Learning how to communicate our thoughts and feelings effectively

through our words directly influences our success and accomplishments in life. It is a learned skill, not a skill we are born with, so as with many other skills, our level of accomplishment relates directly to the importance we give it along with the time and energy we devote to finessing this skill.

It is noteworthy to mention that advances in technology have generated a variety of communication options. I would like to discuss emailing and texting which definitely provide efficient methods to communicate and have an important place in our daily life. However, I would be remiss not to point out that discernment is required when choosing which method of communication to use when sharing "personal" thoughts and feelings. In these instances, we should show respect for the person and circumstances related to our communication. Sometimes, a message in the form of an email or text can be misunderstood, as it is lacking the personal aspect. I have experienced text messages that are cryptic and mysterious as to what they mean. The sender's intention can be confusing. You are left to ponder what the sender was trying to convey. Were they being humorous or sarcastic? What was their intent?

When sharing personal thoughts and feelings, it is deserving of choosing a personal method of communication; the preferred method being an "in person" or "telephone" conversation.

Let's take a moment to reflect on the way that words impact all lives in a such powerful way. Words have the power to touch a heart deeply with love, provide comfort and inspiration, provide courage and strength, bring humor and laughter to a situation, create understanding, impart knowledge. The opportunities are endless. The power of words, the art of communication, can be frivolous or profound. You are the wordsmith, the creator of expressing your thoughts, feelings and ideas. A very exciting concept. Remember, our thoughts create our reality. What you perceive, conceive and believe, you can achieve. Let the essence of your words enhance your life and inspire others.

A parting gem of wisdom: Express appreciation, gratitude, and love for people as you flow through your life journey because life can be fragile. There are no guarantees for tomorrow. Live with no regrets. Don't let the people you love and care about leave this earth without knowing how you feel about them. Appreciation and gratitude is a gift of love from your heart to their heart.

VIGNETTE 10

A Divine Blessing

This juncture of my life relates to when I was approximately forty-eight years old. Thus far, early in life, I had married my high school sweetheart, we were a couple for five years before marriage, married for sixteen years, and had a son together. We divorced in 1983. Subsequent to my divorce, I raised my son and remained close to his dad's family, as they were a cherished part of my life for over twenty years and I loved them as my family. I strongly believe that when a marriage ends and the couple can move on and remain friends, it is the best circumstance to sustain a loving relationship with all family members and this allows life to continue with love being the primary focal point. What is the value of divorcing an entire family as it is a marriage that had ended? It was so important to me to continue to honor the loving bond and relationship we had enjoyed over the years for the sake of my son and all the family members who would also be impacted by this life changing event. I remained close to my in-laws and all family members over the years until, one by one, they were called home. I still love them and miss them to this day. People may pass, but the energy of love remains in our heart, as love never dies. My ex-husband remarried and had two more sons and a daughter with his wife. Although there were some awkward moments in our transition, I am grateful that we were all able to successfully work through those moments. At this point in my life, my mother had passed away. My grandmother had moved in with me following her quadruple heart bypass surgery. My grandmother resided with me for nine years, until she required 24-hour care, at which time it had become a danger for her to be home alone. At this juncture, it was necessary for her to relocate to a nursing facility. During the nine years my grandmother lived with me, it was necessary for me to work two jobs to survive financially, sustain a home, and support the household living expenses for myself, my son and my grandmother. It was a challenging and difficult situation as it required me to sacrifice my social life as a single woman in my mid-thirties. However, I had great determination, strength, and courage to make the senior years of my grandmother's life as comfortable and joyous as possible, as her only child, my mother, had passed away at the young age of forty-eight years old. At this later stage of life, I had dated some, but never made a connection with anyone that was interested in me as a person. What I encountered was the overall interest was in a one-night stand, which was not my cup of tea. The goal for me was to meet someone, become friends, spend time together, learn about one another, and see if a friendship could evolve into an attraction that would develop into a love relationship.

I was genuinely disheartened by the reality of what I discovered in my experience upon reentering the dating scene as a mature woman. Since quality of life is not a value that I am willing to sacrifice, I started to believe that it may be my destiny to live my life without a partner. I was putting deep thought into what my life purpose was and how I was going to move forward alone. I was feeling despair and sadness, but I was also trying to remind myself to "believe" and have "faith" that the future is unknown and that good things manifest and await us when we come from love and not fear.

I have angels in every room in my house to remind me that we are not alone. Love always surrounds us. In my living room, I have two very special angels; One angel says "faith" and one angel says "believe". That serves as a daily reminder that God's love and light surrounds us, even in moments of sadness and disappointment when we are uncertain of the future.

At times, a situation occurs that serves to remind us that blessings are present even in times of crisis and pain. When we make choices that don't have the results we anticipated, we can always make a new choice and move in a new direction. It then becomes a valuable lesson, new wisdom to move forward with. You never know the blessings that await you when you come from love and faith, which leads to the story of my "divine" blessing. God had a surprise in store for me, completely unexpected. A divine blessing I was not anticipating that would rock my world and bless my life in a way that only He could foresee.

Fast forward to April, 1995. It was the day before the Easter Holiday and I had spent the day with my Dad. We met for lunch and had a nice visit. I made plans that evening to meet my dear friend, Francine, for dinner. We planned on eating at the local Indonesian restaurant.

Unbeknownst to me, she and another friend, Olga, arranged a meeting at the restaurant with someone they had known for years, but was unknown to me. Actually, I wasn't aware that this meeting was prearranged. I thought this was just a chance meeting. The truth of our meeting wasn't revealed to me until many years later. My friends thought that we would make a good match, as they had known both Rudy and I for many years, but Rudy and I had never met each other.

So, here we are at the Indonesian restaurant and Rudy comes over to our table to greet my friend, Francine, who introduces him to me. Rudy is invited to join us and, over the course of the evening, he proceeds to tell me his entire life story. My first thought was, my goodness, this man is a talker, I can't get a word in edgewise, which was an unusual trait for a man. I realized upon reflecting back, that he was interested in forming a friendship with me and wanted me to know who he truly was, as a person, so I would be comfortable with him. It wasn't the norm for him to talk incessantly. After dinner, we went back to my friend's house and continued our conversation. I was rolling my eyes in disbelief that someone would tell their entire life story in one evening to someone they just met. When it was time for me to leave, he insisted on following me home in his car to see that I got home safely. I said no thank you, I will be fine. Frankly, as I just met him and didn't know his character, I really didn't want this stranger to know where I lived. He was determined to assure I was safe, so he followed me home anyway. When I discovered he was following me, I actually started driving really fast to try to lose him, but he stayed right behind me. When I pulled up on the block where I lived, there he was, so I said goodnight and waited to go into my house until he pulled away, so he wouldn't know which house I lived in. This became a hilarious memory over the years because Rudy was normally a very cautious driver and did not drive fast. I am sure he thought I was crazy and a speed demon on the road, but apparently it didn't deter him. We continued to become friends and started to meet to go out to eat, which was a joyful experience because we both loved food from a variety of cultures. We married a year later, which, over time, revealed itself to unfold as a divine blessing in my life.

Rudy was a very special and gifted person. Rudy had a heart of gold and radiated unconditional love. We each had a different style. Rudy was calm and very laid back and I was sassy and outgoing. He was a loving, calming influence in my life and I was sassy and added spice to his life. This was an excellent blend upon which to build a joyful, meaningful, and fulfilling relationship. We each had many qualities to share and enhanced the life of one another.

Rudy was deeply spiritual and immeasurably enhanced my spiritual knowledge. Our deep connection and energy together drew people to us. We were both able to help many people through our life experience and knowledge. We developed a rare bond and love that is a "once in a lifetime" connection, truly a gift from God; A divine blessing, which I believe could never be recreated. I believe it was our destiny to be together in this life.

Did we, as human beings, have our disagreements? Absolutely. We both had our own unique way of experiencing life, but we were both honest, loyal, loving people and we had a high regard and unwavering value on coming from truth and love.

We were always honest about our thoughts, ideas, and feelings and we were both very passionate about our beliefs, but we always stood in our truth and, when differences arose, we agreed to respect that we had a different perspective and ultimately agreed to disagree. In all honestly, we both had a stubborn streak. Rudy used to say he was "good" stubborn and he said I was "bad" stubborn. I laughed and pointed out there was no good or bad to being stubborn. It was one in the same, nice try!

Reflections of Love

When we love and are loved, it opens our heart to all the joy life has to offer.

The mystery of the heart is that it grows to accommodate all the love that is given and received.

There are no limits to our capacity to give and receive love. The heart will eternally expand to fulfill our desire to give and receive the blessing of love.

The only way to create love is to be love. Loving thoughts manifest into a loving life and create a more loving world.

VIGNETTE 11

An Extraordinary Life

Before I reveal the story of my husband with you, I would like to acquaint you with the background of his extraordinary life.

There are some people in this world who are a celebration of life and love, and everything that matters most to the heart … Rudy is one of those people. Rudy was born in Makassar on the island of Java, Indonesia to parents, Rosalia and Johan. Rudy's father is of Dutch heritage and was a Captain in the Dutch Army, Tank Division, where he spent much of the war in Burma building the bridge that became famous in the movie "Bridge on the River Kwai". Rudy's mother, Rosalia, was of Belgian heritage.

When Rudy was a small child of about six years old, he and his family became prisoners of war when Japan occupied Indonesia and imprisoned Dutch citizens in prisoner of war camps. Rudy, his mother, sister, and two brothers were separated and put in separate "camps". Food was scarce. Their diet consisted primarily of a small amount of rice. During this time, Rudy witnessed the atrocities of war – hunger, sickness, starvation, death, and children left to wander the streets with no one to care for them after their parents became victims of the war. At an age that, here in the United States, we would be navigating Kindergarten and First Grade, he was bearing witness to suffering, starvation, and death. Rudy had vivid and tragic memories of bodies floating in the river.

Rudy has always had an undying love and deep connection with God. He knew in his heart that those that had suffered the ravages of war and did not survive were no longer suffering. They were now in God's hands, surrounded by the purity of God's loving light and were in a place of pure love, serenity, and peace.

His faith was a source of strength and hope. In his darkest moment of fear for the future, he turned to prayer. He prayed for all those that were suffering, he prayed for peace and love to be restored, the chaos of war to end, and families to be reunited.

At the end of the war, the Red Cross reunited Rudy with his family. Rudy's experience during the war helped to shape him into the compassionate, spiritual individual that he became. Following his release from the prisoner of war camps, Rudy brought home to his mother children that were wandering the streets, dying of dysentery, malnutrition, and starvation; some of which, they were able to save. The war left Rudy with many traumatic memories, but also instilled a strong value to live a life with purpose and a vow to share love and give service to others. Prayer was a strong part of Rudy's daily life for himself, as well as countless others that were suffering a crisis.

When Rudy was about sixteen years old, Indonesia claimed their independence and sent Dutch citizens back to Holland. Rudy spoke

often of how they would ice skate on the frozen canals from city to city in the small country of the Netherlands and how he would stuff his clothing with newspaper to stay warm while riding his bicycle in the freezing weather. Rudy was also a jokester and spoke of the times he would encourage friends to touch their tongue on freezing rails and they would get "stuck" because the moisture would instantly "freeze" their tongue to the railing.

Rudy completed his education in Holland and, as a young adult, joined the Merchant Marines, where he traveled around the world many times over, experiencing different cultures, foods, traditions, and lifestyles. Rudy had a lifetime enjoyment of foods from all cultures and remained forever grateful to have food to eat, as he was well aware of what it was like to experience the pain of hunger.

At about thirty years old, Rudy made the decision to immigrate to the United States, however, he continued to maintain his strong connection to the Dutch Indonesian Community. Rudy loved the joyful music, dancing, and food of the Dutch Indonesian Community. Rudy eventually married, divorced, and worked in a variety of professions. Rudy was especially fond of the time he spent remodeling homes, as he always liked to build and use his carpentry skills.

Rudy met Sarah in the early 1980s and created a home and blended family with Sarah, until Sarah's death in 1992. Rudy remained close to Sarah's children and, when he met me in the Spring of 1995, we became one blended family – Judy, Rudy, Sarah's children and grandchildren and my son, Michael. Our blended family also included Robert (the son of our dear friend Francine) and in August of 2008, we welcomed two granddaughters, Alexandra Jade and Brianna Caitlyn to the family.

Rudy and I relocated to the State of Texas from California in February of 2006, where we made our home in Melissa. We purchased one of the first ten homes in the new Subdivision of North Creek in Melissa. Rudy was the patriarch of the neighborhood where he became friends with the builders, developers, police department, water department, etcetera. Rudy made it a point to greet new neighbors as they moved into the neighborhood and established friendships with many wonderful friends and neighbors. Rudy's garage was like a "Home Depot" of sorts and he freely shared his goods and supplies with neighbors. Rudy became the "go to" man of the subdivision and was sought out for advice, prayers, community resources, and advice on how to solve problems. Rudy had a "heart of gold" and was devoted to helping anyone in need, which included countless hours of prayers, asking God to help those suffering through a "crisis".

Rudy loved to spend time outdoors and he spent the majority of his time in the garden planting fruit, vegetables, and flowers and in the garage working with wood, making tables, benches, children's tables and chair sets. Rudy built furniture to be strong and durable and to stand the test of time much like his relationships. His children's furniture was passed down as the years went by and families grew. Rudy was easily accessible to neighbors for a "chat". Those years were pure joy for Rudy. Rudy also enjoyed a passion for cooking and is well-known for his delicious fried rice, egg rolls, Indonesian sauté, split pea soup with ham, etcetera. Generous by nature, Rudy always cooked for an "army", in order that he could share his good cooking with family, friends, and neighbors. Rudy is remembered for his loving heart, generous nature, and devotion to using his God-given gifts to help others… He never tired of helping people in need.

Rudy and I enjoyed eighteen amazing years together, until his passing in 2013. I will be forever grateful that he graced my life with his unconditional love and for the ways in which his wisdom, life experience, and spiritual enlightenment enhanced my life. Rudy was a truly a divine blessing in my life and I thank God for this extraordinary gift of love.

I wrote this heartfelt poem in loving memory of Rudy after his passing and want to share this poem with you.

A Legacy of Love

Your words are like flowers,

Soft as a breeze, as deep as the sea,

Reflections of the love you have for me.

My spirit is light,

My heart warmed by love,

Thoughts flood my mind,

With visions of our love.

Timeless with grace,

An eternal flame now,

Lights my world, as I try to find my way,

Without you in my physical space.

May God surround you with his light and love and hold you in His grace.

I will be forever blessed by the glow of our love, the spark and essence of our energy, our life together as one.

May God smile upon both of us as we embrace our new life, as love never dies, but continues its forever glow.

                                                  Love, Judy

I believe that our connection to others is the essence of life and directly relates to our life purpose. How we treat people and interact with others in our daily life reflects the essence of who we are, our true authentic self.

I would like to share some excerpts of testimonials received for Rudy by friends that were touched by his life:

We all loved Rudy and his wonderful spirit. You could never be sad in his presence because he was so full of joy, love, and positive energy.

> I hope you don't mind me sharing this with you... After my father passed away, Rudy greeted me by saying "Congratulations on the passing of your Dad". I was initially taken aback, but quickly realized that it was the best greeting that anyone could have given me. Our ultimate goal in life should be to live a life pleasing to Christ and strive to achieve the winning prize of going to heaven. We will miss our dear friend, but I know he is in heaven now enjoying his rewards.
>
> **Katrice B.**

> You and Rudy have very special granddaughters that touched my heart. I know he will always be with you, watching over you, and protecting you. He was an amazing man and touched the lives of many people. What a great example of how we should all live. I'm honored to have known him and to call you both my friends.
>
> **Sherry R.**

> I remember Rudy and the abiding love he had for you and the love you had for one another. You are both such a strong, spiritual couple.
>
> **Jacqueline L.**

I would like to share that the evening before Rudy passed, that his little granddaughters, Alexandra and Brianna, wanted to talk to their "Opa". Their daddy said that Opa was sick and would be an angel soon. You can talk to Opa, but he can't talk with you, but he can <u>hear</u> you. So, they rang through on the cell phone, which we put on speaker phone and held it close to Rudy's ear. The last words Rudy heard that night were the voices of his granddaughters. They said "Hi Opa, we love you. Go to God Opa, don't be afraid". A powerful message from two little girls that are four and a half years old. They love their Opa and their Opa dearly loved those little girls. That love lives on through savored memories of times shared and transcend life ~ The essence of an enduring love.

Rudy's last words to me, before lapsing into a coma that night, were, "I love you very much, thank you for all you did for me, and for loving me. I will be back (to visit). I will *always* be with you".

The Legend of Hummingbirds

Legends say that hummingbirds float free of time, carrying our hopes of love, joy, and celebration. The hummingbird's delicate grace reminds us that life is rich, beauty is everywhere, every personal connection has meaning, and love and laughter is life's sweetest creation.

Author Unknown

VIGNETTE 12

A Divine Gift

Rudy's story begins in July of 1937 in Makassar on the Island of Java, Indonesia. Rudy's father, Johan, is in the Dutch army and his wife Rosalia is giving birth to their new baby son, Rudy. It is a very difficult birth and their baby is born encased in a chrysalis; a very rare occurrence called a "veiled" birth. By current statistics, this occurs in approximately one out of 80,000 vaginal births. In this type of birth, the baby is born fully encased in the amniotic sac, also called an "En Caul" birth. The sac is not broken and the amniotic fluid is not released until the baby is outside of the womb.

Rudy is bleeding profusely where the umbilical cord was attached and they are watching him closely and are gravely concerned as there is a strong possibility that this bleeding is endangering his life and he may not survive.

Rudy's mother Rosalia, is suffering overwhelming worry and concern. She cannot sleep and is diligently watching over him, praying for him to live, when suddenly she receives a visitation by an Angelic Being, radiating a bright light. This Angelic Being was sent to bring her a message. The Angelic Being told her how to care for Rudy and cleanse him. She was told that if she did this, her child would live. In this message, the Angelic Being shared with her that Rudy was a special child. He had been blessed with a special and unique gift, which would grow stronger over the passage of time. Rosalia faithfully followed the instructions she was given by the Angelic Being and Rudy healed and began to thrive.

The "divine gift" that God bestowed on Rudy was the ability to see and communicate telepathically with souls that had passed, crossed over to the other side.

I would like to share with you that when we cross over, the essence of our life force energy, or soul, detaches from the human body that we used in this life. The human body, at some point, will no longer be able to sustain life, but at the time of our death, our soul detaches from the human body. The energy of our soul does not die, it just changes form and lives on in a different form, in an ascended dimension. As energy does not die, in reality, our soul transitions to another dimension, heaven, and we return to our source, our Creator. The energy, love, and connection that we have for our loved ones here on earth never dies. The essence of our higher self, which is unique to each one of us, stays with us. During our lifetime, we have experiences and learn lessons that add to our wisdom and soul knowledge, which raises our vibration and enhances our celestial wisdom, which will be invaluable in helping others from the other side. After transitioning to the other side, we continue to use our loving energy and wisdom to help people here on earth navigate through the challenges that they encounter throughout their life journey.

As a soul, we have the ability to visit loved ones. We continue to bless others by radiating our loving energy as we visit our loved ones, especially in times of crisis. As a soul, we radiate loving light and surround our loved ones with loving energy to bring them comfort, strength, and hope. However, as a soul, we also share joyous occasions with loved ones here on earth, such as a wedding, birth of a baby, or an amazing accomplishment or milestone deserving of celebration. In essence, we watch over our loved ones, nurture them, and sustain our loving connection with them throughout their life journey. We are also there to meet them and help to guide them when it is their time to be called home.

When we pass, we are surrounded by angels and met by loved ones who have passed before us and we are encompassed by a bright, radiant light; as described by those that have had a near-death experience (NDE), been pronounced clinically dead, but lived to share their experience.

This radiant light immerses our soul in such profound pure love and joy that it leaves no doubt that it could only come from God, our Creator. This feeling of love is so profound, that there are no words magnificent enough to describe this feeling. Everyone who has experienced the beauty of God's light and love does not want to return to their human body, but some people have not completed what they came here to do, and must return to earth to finish their work here. Those that have experienced an NDE, state unequivocally that they no longer fear death.

After passing, we all experience a life review, where we are visually shown a review of how we lived our life. This is a review of the choices and decisions we made, and how our treatment and interactions with other human beings affected others. During this life review, we actually feel the emotions that others felt as the recipient of our choices and actions. The sole purpose of this life review is for learning and clarity and is not designed to serve as punishment. What we do not understand here on earth, we are blessed with the gift of clarity and understanding after we pass, so we can move forward as an enlightened soul.

Twenty years before I met Rudy, I personally experienced a visitation by my mother after her passing. In my visitation, she appeared as a mist floating above me. I intrinsically knew she was there to show her love for me. As an adult, my son had a visitation by his Great Grandmother after her passing, before he became aware of her passing, or had been notified that she had crossed over. She shared a message of her love and support. My son was aware of her presence and received her message telepathically. He also felt the deep love she had for him and he was grateful for her visit.

After I met Rudy, and at the point we knew that we would become husband and wife, he revealed the details of his unique gift to me. I immediately thought it was an amazing blessing, but Rudy also shared that it could be a burden at times because he was constantly surrounded by souls anxious to communicate with him, as they could see he had the ability to see them and hear their messages telepathically. He had to learn how to protect his energy by sometimes consciously closing off his ability to receive these communications.

It is also important to note that Rudy had this unique gift at a time in history where a large majority of people were ultra-conservative in their personal and religious beliefs. These beliefs are taught to us here on earth and passed down over generations. We are not born with these philosophies, but are taught by our parents, family, religious affiliations, and other influences growing up.

In the 1930s, many people were taught that this type of ability was the work of the devil and they were not open to the concept that it was a divine gift from God, as it was not tangible and it wasn't comfortable for people to believe what could not be proven and strongly conflicted with the beliefs they were taught and grew up believing. Consequently, Rudy was not free to share or discuss his gift with others. Very few people knew of his abilities, except when he was called upon to deliver an important message, at which time he blessed the life of the recipient with the intended message from their loved one.

Part of the reason I am sharing in detail what I have learned throughout my life journey is to impart knowledge and honor Rudy's amazing gift. I know Rudy is free now, surrounded by God's love and light, but I would like to share his God given abilities and experiences to set him free here on earth in a way that he wasn't able to do freely during his lifetime. I am his voice to share "some" of these moments and stories with you as there are too many to present that occurred over the course of his seventy-five years on earth. I know his light is shining bright as he continues to use his celestial wisdom and knowledge to bless others from the heavens above. Rudy is especially remembered for being deeply spiritual, for his kind and loving heart, and the "unconditional" love that he radiated to others.

As you can see from the previous segment I wrote on his extraordinary life, he also experienced tremendous suffering during his life, but he chose to rise above that and used those painful experiences to aspire to do good in this world and live a life of giving service to others.

One of the first things Rudy shared with me was that, as a child, he thought everyone could see what he was able to see. It took years for him to discover that the ability to see and communicate with souls on the other side was unique to him. When he tried to share these experiences with others, their reaction was one of disdain and disbelief; except for his mother who always lovingly understood and accepted his special gift.

VIGNETTE 13

Messages of Love

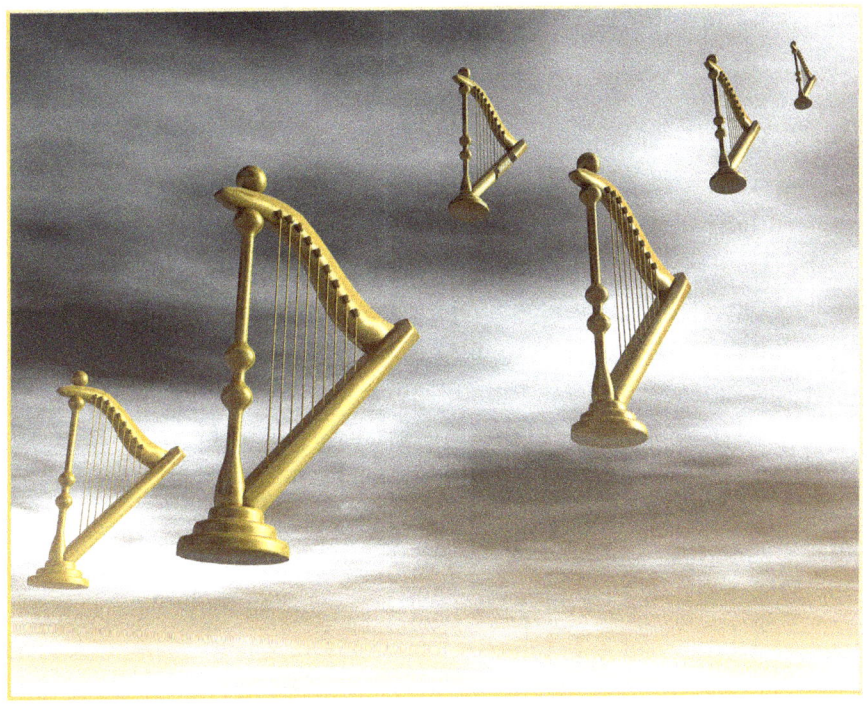

I would like to share some memories with you of how Rudy used his divine gift to bless people with messages of love.

1. One of the first experiences Rudy shared with me was when he attended a funeral of a long-time friend. Rudy said he always dreaded going to funerals because not only is he grieving the physical loss of the person who passed, but that person attends

their own funeral, as a soul, and always communicates with him as they can recognize his special ability to see and hear them telepathically. In this instance, his friend had a very special request for him to pass on an important message to a family member. This situation was always highly emotional for Rudy as it takes an immense amount of energy to engage and communicate with a soul that has passed. His friend told Rudy to have his loved one look in a particular jacket in a specific pocket to retrieve information he had written on a note but wasn't able to deliver before his passing. Rudy passed the message to the family member, as requested. The family member was in disbelief, but said they would check the jacket when they arrived home. They later contacted Rudy and advised they found the note. The note had information and a message that related to a life-changing decision the family member was making to go to Seminary School to become a Minister. He stated the information and message was encouraging him to follow this path and dedicate his life to God. The message from his loved one gave him the strength and courage to follow this path and move forward with the study of Theology to serve God and mankind. A beautiful legacy and an amazing way for Rudy to use the give God had bestowed upon him.

2. An ethereal experience I personally had with Rudy was after we had recently married and were relaxing at home. Rudy said, "Your mother is here. (my mother had passed away twenty years prior to this date). He said she is so happy we are together and she said to tell your sister it _was_ her." I was shocked. The incident my mother was referring to was one afternoon when my sister was working alone in a small collectible shop. A man came into the shop, determined that she was alone, held a knife to her throat, robbed the register, and had her show him where the money was in the back office. He was preparing to rape her

and suddenly and unexpectedly asked if that was her wedding ring she was wearing. My sister said, "Yes, it is", but that day she was actually wearing my mother's wedding ring. He was agitated and nervous and abruptly left the shop without taking the ring or harming her. My sister ran outside for help and saw a bright beam of light stream across the sky. She told me, at the time, that she thought it was Mom and that somehow Mom's presence and energy had protected her from being raped and assaulted. This situation had occurred a couple of years before I met Rudy and I had <u>never</u> told him about it. My mother wanted my sister to know that she was with her that day. An amazing revelation; the streak of light she saw was Mom leaving after she knew that my sister was safe.

3. Rudy and I were invited to attend a holiday get together at the home of one of the Executives I worked for. Rudy had not personally met any of the people I worked with, so this would be his first opportunity to meet and chat with people I connected with on a daily basis in my work environment.

The hostess of the party was one of the Executives I worked for who was of Asian heritage, who I would discover was originally born in Taiwan. At this point in time, I knew little of her personal background or life story, but as the years progressed, we would become very dear friends. In addition to her co-workers, she had also invited family members and friends to join the holiday party celebration.

Her husband was mixing apple martinis that were absolutely awesome. I didn't drink very often but, on special occasions, I did enjoy a cocktail. We were chatting about her husband's talents as a bartender when Rudy said to her, "Your father is here and he is in his military uniform. He asked me to say thank you to your mother and her husband for doing such a wonderful job of raising you. He said he is very grateful".

Her reaction to the message was one of shock and surprise. She immediately went to the other room to get her mother. When she returned with her mother, she asked Rudy to repeat the message and describe the military uniform he was wearing. Rudy shared her father's message of gratitude and described in detail what the uniform looked like. She and her mother then explained that her father had passed when she was a very young child in some type of military confrontation, and she was too young to have a memory of him. After his passing, her mother had eventually remarried and relocated to the United States. Rudy told her that her father states that your mother has a photo of him in this uniform. They were discussing this information in Mandarin Chinese, her mother's native language. My boss then stated that her mother explained that her sister took all of the old photos and she no longer has them at her house. Her father, again, assured her mother that she has the photo in her possession of him in his military uniform. They thanked Rudy for relating the heart-warming message and we moved on to other conversations, primarily focusing on Rudy's unique gift, as they had many questions about his abilities.

A few days later, her mother called to tell her that she woke up early that morning and was compelled to open a dresser drawer that she normally doesn't access, and there was the photo of her father in his military uniform, exactly as Rudy had described. Her mother gave her daughter, my boss, the photo, and it became a very special keepsake for her in memory of her father and his loving message.

4. My Grandmother was named Frances, but as a child, she was affectionately called "Dottie" by her family. Her birth was a

delightful surprise to her parents, as they had tried for years to get pregnant with no success. When they gave up and tried to accept that they would not be blessed with a child, she became their most treasured surprise package. Needless to say, my grandmother was doted over by both parents.

In my Grandmother's later years, after the passing of her daughter at the young age of forty-eight years old, and quadruple heart bypass surgery, she resided with me for over nine years. When it became necessary for her to have care around the clock, she was relocated to a nursing care facility.

My son was delighted to get an adorable new Pomeranian puppy, whom he named "Dottie" in honor of my Grandmother and her feisty personality. We were excited for my Grandmother to meet her namesake, so the entire family arranged a visit to introduce the puppy to her at the nursing care facility. My Grandmother was overjoyed and flattered that my son would honor her in his way. It was a very joyful visit and, whenever we would visit her, she would always ask about Dottie.

In January 2000, just after the transition to the Twenty-First Century, my Grandmother passed away at the age of ninety-two. I often thought it was remarkable that she came into this world with much celebration as an unexpected surprise in 1907 and lived long enough to celebrate the dawn of the Twenty-First Century, extraordinary.

Strangely, and unexpectedly, my son's dog " Dottie," passed away within twenty-four hours of my Grandmother, even though she was still young and did not show signs of being ill. We concluded that my Grandmother and Dottie had such a deep, soul connection that they chose to transition together.

Rudy and I were visiting my son's house after the passing of my Grandmother and Dottie when Rudy suddenly said he saw

Dottie, as a soul, visiting their home following her passing, a sign of love and her final goodbye.

Yes, our love and connection with our pets also carries over into the afterlife. This is so heartwarming and an amazing revelation and discovery. Loved ones and pets visit us after death and are deeply devoted to remaining connected to us from the hereafter.

I believe that we continue our unique connection to others in this life until our last breath. The essence of "who we are" continues to impact the lives of others until we are called home. We aren't usually aware of how we impact the lives of others, but I would like to share an example of one such experience with you.

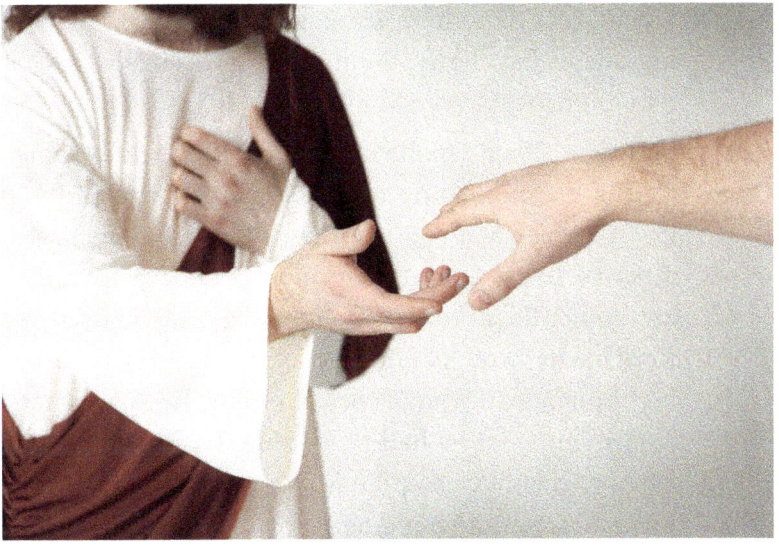

When my husband Rudy was in hospice care when he was nearing the end of his life journey, I was asking God why good and loving people must suffer through the effects and discomfort of disease. I believe that our unique qualities and gifts are still influential in impacting those around us, as we can still reflect our love, kindness, gratitude, strength, courage, and inspiration to others. However, it is difficult to see past the end of life experience and sadness brought about by the knowledge that our loved one will soon be leaving our physical world. The mind is flooded with so many different thoughts, feelings, and emotions that are intensified by the impact of this impending loss.

The hospice team that was caring for Rudy was so amazing. I had immense gratitude that they would choose to lovingly help people through the last stage of their life.

There was a special person that Rudy looked forward to seeing every day that he seemed to have a special connection with. Her name was Sara, but Rudy called her Stephanie, from day one. She helped to bathe him and understood his Dutch accent. So, when there was confusion over what Rudy was saying, she would clarify. Sometimes, it was hilarious what people thought he was saying.

Sara was a single mother of five children and was highly energetic. One day, Rudy took hold of her arm and said, "Slow down". Sara later told me that she deeply understood Rudy's message. It was a very timely message and was extremely important to her life at that moment. After Rudy passed, Sara and I were having a telephone conversation and she shared with me her thoughts on what a special person Rudy was and what an amazing impact he had on her life. I said I didn't understand why he called her Stephanie and not her given name of Sara. I was constantly reminding Rudy that her name was Sara, not Stephanie. Sara revealed that at the time of her birth she was to be given the name of Stephanie, but something prompted the name change at the very last moment. She stated that she was not told why the name was changed or what the reason for the name change was. Sara also stated that Rudy knew her mother was an alcoholic. This was a fact that she had <u>never</u> shared with anyone. God had just given me the gift of confirmation of how we continue to affect the lives of others until our last breath. Sara said she would always remember Rudy and the ways in which his wisdom enriched her life. Amen.

There are so many ways that we share loving energy with others. Sometimes, it is through wise words. Sometimes, quiet strength speaks louder than words.

> ***"Hearts often understand in ways
> that minds cannot".***

VIGNETTE 14

Energy, the Gift of Life

You must <u>be</u> what you want to attract.

This passage was inspired by a conversation I had with my two granddaughters, Alexandra and Brianna, who are, at the time of this writing, fifteen years old. We treasure our time together and find great joy in our "girl chats".

We were having a conversation about the Universe and how all living thigs radiate and vibrate with energy. We <u>are</u> energy! People, animals, birds, fish, trees, grass, plants, flowers, all of nature. Energy never dies, it just changes form. That is the cycle of life. Life is energy and we are all connected by the life force of that energy.

As human beings, we must understand that we were given the gift of life. The energy of life comes in all shapes, sizes, colors, forms, and cultures, yet we are all infinitely connected.

How we evolve, the experiences we have, how we choose to use our energy, and what we learn on our life journey will impact our planet, our Universe, and life at this moment and in the future.

As human beings, we must embrace nature. We must nourish, nurture, respect, and protect our world to sustain the balance of life and make choices that are not destructive to our eco systems and our planet. Choosing to nourish, nurture, respect, and protect our planet impacts the air we breathe, the water we drink, the food we eat, and life itself. The choices we make on a daily basis matter. We have the potential and wisdom to recognize how our collective energy can empower and inspire choices that come from an open mind, an open heart, love and light, and the desire to do no harm.

Envision the gift of life as an exquisitely wrapped package. This extraordinary gift comes in all shapes, sizes, colors, and cultures. This celestial gift is created and given life with pure love and light. From birth, our journey begins. Please understand that we are pure love, energy, and light at birth. We do not come into this world with any negativity or prejudice. We are open in mind, spirit, and heart.

All of us have unique gifts to share and we have the capacity to blossom at any point along our life journey. It is a journey of discovering what we are passionate about and choosing where we want to use our energy and how we want to live our life.

We all have different circumstances, different experiences, and different influences. As we live life, we will have many choices to make.

Please understand and embrace the fact that no one limits you. Only you have the power to limit yourself, if you so choose. The other side of the spectrum is that you absolutely have the ability to empower yourself by making high vibrational choices, which come from love, light, and truth.

You must <u>be</u> what you want to attract. If you want to be loved, you must be loving. If you want to be treated with kindness and respect, you must treat others with kindness and respect. Give thought to the qualities that you love <u>most</u> in others, then <u>be</u> that person.

The energy you radiate to others is what you will attract to your life. That is how the energy of the Universe works, known as the law of attraction.

At the other end of the spectrum, we have low vibrational energies, which include anger, resentment, deceit, selfishness, a lack of concern for the way that we interact with and treat others, and the hurt and pain that these choices inflict on others that are receiving this energy. If low vibrational energy is what you are radiating, this too is the energy you will attract to your life.

The way you use your energy and the choices you make is in your hands. Embrace and take responsibility for the choices you make, as the experience that accompanies these choices is also uniquely yours.

The amazing thing about life is that making a mistake does not define your life. You always have the ability to choose a new path, connect with your higher self, and open your mind and heart to come from love and light.

Remember, if you focus on the hurt from an experience, you will continue to feel the pain. If you focus on the lesson you have learned from an experience, you will move forward with wisdom and continue to grow and flourish.

I would like to share an inspirational message from the Kuan Yin Oracle Deck, by Alana Fairchild. This Oracle Deck was a gift from a dear friend.

In the Buddhist religion, Kuan Yin is the goddess of compassion and healing. Although I am not Buddhist, I draw inspiration and wisdom from all cultures.

Before drawing a card from this deck, I said a prayer and asked the Goddess Kuan Yin what inspirational message she would like to share with the world today.

I drew Card #13, "Hear the Yellow Tiger Mother".

For those of you that are interested in numerology, thirteen reduces down to Number Four. The Number Four connects mind, body, and spirit with the physical world to build a solid foundation of beliefs, values, unconditional love, compassion, and joy. Amazingly, it aligns perfectly with this message. Goddess Kuan Yin has this inspirational message for us:

> *"Sometimes we must be strong and hold true whilst all around us seems to be shifting and changing. The Yellow Tiger Mother, Kuan Yin, in her Guardian role, is roaring her divine sound within you.*
>
> *She asks you to hear her, to remember that you are a powerful being of light and even whilst you are in flow with universal forces, your strong roots help you be at peace with your truth, standing your ground while your light shines true.*
>
> *You are more powerful, strong, and courageous than you realize. Your strength is not stubbornness or resistance. It is holding firm to what you feel in your heart to be true and, in time, you will come to realize the wisdom of your courage. Your strength at this time is needed, like a protective shield providing nurturing to a young plant. Your strength and refusal to be dissuaded from your truth helps your dreams and higher path continue to manifest.*
>
> *Allow yourself to hear the Yellow Tiger Mother as she gifts you with power, strength, and knowing. Be brave and stay true to yourself, beloved".*

Wishing you love and light. Let your light shine bright!

VIGNETTE 15

Reflections of Love

The essence of life is love. Our purpose in life is to learn to love and love to learn.

Love immeasurably enriches our lives and manifests itself in so many ways. When we think about love, the first thought that comes to mind is romantic love, the love of a spouse or life partner, and the deep love we have for our children and family.

God also bestows love, light, and the grace of kindness among all people that are a part of our daily life. Often times, these souls are strangers, earthly angels that walk among us.

An act of kindness is an act of love. A moment that comes from the heart, is unselfish, and is freely given, with no expectation of anything in return. As a human being, we all need to be seen and heard in this life. Our thoughts and feelings need validation that "we matter" and that we have unique qualities to share that add value and purpose to our life and others. Those moments in life when we let the light of our soul shine bright, reflects the very essence of the way in which we are all connected in this world and Universe.

We must never underestimate an act of kindness, no matter how small. Sometimes, we are so busy trying to navigate our life, that we don't take the time to give thought to what others may be experiencing and coping with in life.

Let's explore that thought for a moment. Can you recollect a time when you were stressed or depressed, feeling that life was almost too overwhelming to navigate? Then, perhaps you went to the store, and a stranger opened the door for you, nodded to you as they passed you down the aisle, said hello, had a short chat with you, or graciously let you go ahead of them in the checkout area? These are heartwarming examples of how you were just validated, soul to soul. You then left the store feeling uplifted in spirit and soul.

These examples of uplifting encounters are a part of what makes life worth living. We should all strive to engage in acts of kindness every day. Be a light for yourself and others whenever, wherever, and as often as possible.

It is amazing how we have the power to choose to radiate our energy to grace the life of others with the gift of kindness and respect. Choose to be a light in this world. Radiate your love and light. Personify a beautiful example of a human being that is kind and gracious to others.

These moments of kindness are an inspiration to mankind, illuminate the good in this world, and raise the vibration of joy and loving energy in the Universe.

I have immense gratitude for all people that connect with their higher self, come from their heart and soul with love, and give of themselves. Those that give their time, messages of encouragement, wisdom, energy, hope, strength, and faith. These acts of kindness are messages of love.

Sometimes, love is not spoken in words, but is just as powerful. Those poignant moments when someone sits with you, or holds your hand, in a time of crisis with love and silent strength. There are times that we have no words, but we show the depth of our love in quiet support. Sometimes, hearts understand what we are unable to express in words.

The essence of love engages all of our senses; touch, smell, hearing, feeling and taste. Love and memories are infinitely connected to all our senses. Sights, sounds, smells, touch, and taste can instantly trigger a heartwarming memory, a moment in time that transports us back to a sentimental memory that is forever a cherished part of our heart.

I vividly remember the sweet fragrance of my grandmother growing up; the beautiful aroma of flowers. It takes me back to how I felt so much love for her and I envision the love and warmth I felt when she hugged me. I could "feel" her love.

The beauty and aromatic fragrance of flowers is also deeply connected to loving memories of my mother. When I grew up, people cultivated beautiful gardens. Gardens are a very Zen place for me. I always marvel at the great beauty of all that God has created. We always had flowers in my home growing up, displayed in a bouquet or, often times, my mother would float Camelias or Gardenias from our garden in a beautiful bowl. The aroma was heavenly. Every Spring and Summer, my mother planted Sweet Pea seeds along a small fence across the center of our back yard. The more you harvest Sweet Peas, the more flowers they produce. Their beauty and fragrance is heavenly and their aroma filled our living room. Love blooms in many ways.

One especially heartwarming, sweet memory deep in my heart and soul is of my husband Rudy. Rudy used to wear the fragrance Polo by Ralph Lauren. It was his signature fragrance. I can't even describe how amazing this fragrance blended with the warmth and energy of his unconditional love. After he passed, I kept a bottle of his Polo cologne. I open it at times when I want to "immerse" myself in the deep love and memories we share. Our two granddaughters were four years old when he passed. One time, when they had a sleepover at my house, I asked them to close their eyes and tell me what this aroma makes them think of. They both immediately shrieked, "Opa!"

These are just a few examples of how the sense of smell is such a powerful connection to the window of our soul and the memories therein.

Another beautiful example externally connected to our sense of sight, sound, and smell is linked to that moment when we step into the home of a person hosting a special event. Instantly, we are immersed in the heavenly aroma of divine cuisine. The smell of roasted turkey, cinnamon, fresh baked pies, fresh baked bread, freshly brewed coffee, etcetera. We all cherish those special and gifted people in our life that are skilled in the art of cooking. Every holiday and special occasion in our life is directly connected to the people that prepare incredibly delicious dishes from the depth of their heart and soul, infusing their creations with love. This is truly an amazing gift and blessing given and received from one heart to another.

The joy of reliving these heartwarming memories never diminish over time but, in reality, are savored through reminiscing with family and friends.

Music is one of the most profound illustrations of an experience that directly touches our heart and soul through the pure joy of sound, harmony, vibration, and rhythm. You hear it, feel it, and move with it. The experience is all encompassing for our senses. We receive the tremendous joy of music deep in our soul. It engages us in a multitude of thoughts, feelings, and emotions. Hearing a song can instantly take us back to a heartwarming, cherished memory, feeling the emotion of where you were, what you were doing, and how you felt.

As all living things vibrate with the energy of life and are infinitely connected, I want to share a delightful discovery I made on YouTube. If you open the YouTube App and type "Animals reacting to music" in the search bar, it will pull up fascinating videos of a variety of wild animals in their natural habitat responding to artists playing a wide-ranging array of musical instruments. I often watch and enjoy these videos with my granddaughters. We are in awe at the depth of intelligence and emotion that the animals display.

I would like to share a special series of videos by Paul Barton, filmed in Thailand on an Elephant Preserve. Mr. Barton is a classical pianist and he takes his piano out into the Preserve and plays classical music for the elephants. It is astounding to me that these massive animals with such high intelligence, are completely mesmerized by the music. The elephants stand, listen, move to the music, and even get tears in their eyes while listening to the creative genius of Beethoven, Mozart, Bach, etcetera.

Open your heart, mind, and senses to all the ways in which love is present in our lives. Music and love are two things in life that supersede language barriers, touch people's heart and soul, and is universal to all cultures. All people recognize love and kindness and find great joy and appreciation for music, even if verbal communication is not possible because they speak a different language.

With all the ways in which our world has evolved over the last seventy-five plus years since my birth, there is one notable shift in the evolution of mankind that I welcome with open arms and an open heart. That magnificent shift that is taking place is living life in a more inclusive world.

Reflect on the fact that we are born of pure love and light. We are not born into this world with any prejudice or negativity. Those beliefs are learned here on Earth. If we come into this life with pure love and light in mind, body, heart, and soul, that is confirmation and affirmation to me that our Creator intended for us to be open in mind, heart, soul, and spirit. Life is preordained to be inclusive of all cultures, nationalities, religions, and ways of living life in our world.

Love and our connection to others, and all living things, is the essence of life. There is capacity in this world to accommodate a multitude of beliefs, philosophies, and ways in which to live life. A world in which we embrace one another as human beings is a world of infinite possibilities and amazing opportunities to experience life, learn, and grow in wisdom. There is a place to be respectful of differences, as well as a place to find comfort in that with which we are familiar.

Families and friendships are a beautiful example that illuminate the way in which people are opening their minds and hearts to be inclusive of all cultures, religions, and beliefs. This is a shift that will immeasurably enrich life for mankind. We are in the transitional process of opening our minds and hearts to accept that love is not limited. Love is beautiful in all of the ways it exists and is expressed. Families are now blended, multi-cultural, and friendships often become part of our family unit with love at the core of what is the most important element in living a fulfilling and rewarding life.

At the end of life, we understand that our journey was all about love and our connection to one another and all living things. We will feel immense gratitude for all the ways that love has graced our life. In the end, "love" is all that matters.

VIGNETTE 16

Garden of Inspiration

Reflect on Life as a Beautiful Garden

Reflections of life as a beautiful garden.

We plant seeds, watch it blossom, flourish, and grow,

Weather the seasons of change,

Add fresh ideas and nourish with new wisdom, beliefs, and philosophies,

Weed out what doesn't work for our greater good,

Find joy and inspiration in the ever-changing beauty of our garden,

Look forward to new growth, new energy, and the enduring joy of a garden well-tended.

May your garden flourish and reward you with great inspiration and joy, as you follow your unique path leading to enlightenment and reaping the gems of wisdom that unfold throughout your journey to discovering your authentic self and the true meaning of life.

May you experience many blessings on your path to enlightenment and great joy in the creation of your special and unique "Garden of Life".

—**Judy White-Artz**

The Inspiration of Intentions

Life is like a river, ever flowing. Sometimes, we experience smooth water and, at times, we experience rough waters, but we must remember that new adventures, experiences, and blessings await us around every bend, eager for us to explore and discover what lies ahead.

I would like to share an invaluable tool that I use for inspiration and to focus my thoughts to guide my energy into what I am most passionate about in life. Writing down my intentions channels my energy into what I aspire to manifest that reflects what I wish to accomplish and achieve on my life journey. **Please Note:** I created a special Journal at the back of this book for you, the reader, to note your most private thoughts in a confidential space. This space includes pages for you to make note of your *Intentions*, what you have *Gratitude* for, your *Thoughts*, and your *Feelings*.

My Intentions

1. To be a small "light" in this World, to radiate positive, loving energy into the Universe.
2. To radiate and spread love, inspiration, positivity, kindness, and hope.
3. To finish and publish my book that will, hopefully, inspire others on their life journey.
4. To accept that life is different from my idea of what is "comfortable" for me.
5. To grow in wisdom when I am faced with experiences that bring me difficulty, stress, and challenges.
6. To remember that I can accomplish whatever I choose to use my energy to create.
7. To have more tolerance and acceptance of "what is" in life, as opposed to disappointment over what I project it should be. Move forward in life with "what is" so.
8. To remember that God loves me even though, at times, I may feel alone.

Mantra

Today, I will choose happiness.

I have everlasting faith in my journey.

Every experience is helping me to grow and evolve into someone I can be proud of.

Every day is a new beginning, with new opportunities.

I will stop thinking about what could have been or what should have been said or done.

When I choose to see the good in others, I will illuminate the good in myself.

I will be <u>Strong</u> enough to let go of what does not serve me,

<u>Wise</u> enough to move forward.

<u>Hones</u>t enough to work hard,

<u>Patien</u>t enough to wait for the blessings I have earned throughout my journey.

Gems of Wisdom for Living Life

Within My Control

- My thoughts, choices, and actions
- The goals I set
- What I choose to give my energy to
- How I respond to challenges
- The boundaries I set

Beyond My Control

- The past
- The future
- The actions of other people
- The opinions of other people
- What happens around me
- What other people think of me
- How other people choose to take care of themselves

What you "Seek" in Life, you will Find

Be a Seeker . . . . . .

A Seeker of Love and Kindness

> *Radiate Love and Kindness*

A Seeker of Joy and Happiness

> *Radiate Joy and Happiness*

A Seeker of Knowledge and Wisdom

> *Radiate Knowledge and Wisdom*

A Seeker of Positivity

        Radiate Positivity

A Seeker of Strength and Courage

        Radiate Strength and Courage

A Seeker of Faith and Hope

        Radiate Faith and Hope

A Seeker of Peace and Compassion

        Radiate Peace and Compassion

'BE' THE ENERGY OF WHAT YOU WANT TO ATTRACT

Potpourri of Inspirational Thoughts

Hearts often understand in ways the mind cannot comprehend.

Love is an act of faith and courage.

Cry, Forgive, Learn, Move on.

Let your tears water the seeds of your future happiness.

Author Unknown

If you continue to focus on the *Pain*, you will continue to feel and experience the hurt.

If you focus on the *Lesson*, you will continue to grow in wisdom and move forward in life.

Joy, Love, and Positivity need to be nurtured.

Positivity sparks joy and creativity.

I would rather adjust my life to your absence, than adjust my boundaries to accommodate your disrespect.

Author Unknown

If you **surrender** completely to the moments as they pass, you **live** more richly in those moments.

Reach high, for stars lie hidden in your soul.

Dream deep, for every dream precedes the goal.

Independence is happiness.

Instead of giving myself reason why I can't, I give myself reasons why I can.

At times, our own **light** goes out and is rekindled by a **spark** from another person.

Author Unknown

People are like stained glass ***windows***.

They sparkle and ***shine*** when the sun is out, but when the darkness sets in,

Their true ***beauty*** is revealed, only if there is a light from within.

In order to succeed, we must first ***believe*** that we can.

When walking through the "valley of shadows", remember, a shadow is cast by ***light***.

Author Unknown

The Power of Words

Your Thoughts and Words Shape your World

Words are powerful. Once you say them, you cannot take them back.

So, choose wisely. "Think first" what you want your message to be.

If you act in an irrational manner, the focus will be on your "behavior" and <u>not</u> your message.

The goal is to deliver your message in a way that can be received and considered without shifting the attention to your behavior.

Success of delivering your message lies in thought and presentation.

The true power of words is to deliver a meaningful message.

A wise person accepts responsibility to deliver a meaningful message.

A fool believes that they are entitled to speak without the wisdom of forethought, leaving no doubt that their message is self-serving and lacks in value.

The true value and power of communication is in the exchange of intelligent thoughts, beliefs and ideas.

—Judy White-Artz

A Loving Heart and Soul

When we love and are loved, it opens our heart to all the joy life has to offer.

The mystery of the heart is that it grows to accommodate all the love that is given and received.

There are no limits to our capacity to give and receive love. The heart will eternally expand to fulfill our desire to give and receive the blessing of love.

The only way to create love is to be love.

Loving thoughts manifest into a loving life and create a more loving world.

—**Judy White-Artz**

Heart to Heart

Sometimes in this lifetime,

We meet a special soul,

Who fills our very essence,

To almost overflow.

We drink the cup of friendship,

It tastes like ruby wine,

And you know within your heart,

This meeting was divine.

This soul that lives within your heart,

No distance can prevail,

An inner spark, within the heart,

Becomes a Holy Grail.

The beginning of a journey,

In which you both shall be,

A reflection of each other,

For all eternity.

—**Lilaneyah**

This is my wish for you;

Comfort on difficult days,

Smiles when sadness intrudes,

Rainbows to follow the clouds,

Laughter to kiss your lips,

Sunsets to warm your heart,

Hugs when spirits sag,

Beauty for your eyes to see,

Friendships to brighten your being,

Faith so that you can believe,

Confidence for when you doubt,

Courage to know yourself,

Patience to accept the truth,

Love to complete your life.

—**Ralph Waldo Emerson**

About Judy White-Artz

Judy White-Artz is an empath. People have long been drawn to her loving, healing energy, easily sharing their life stories and seeking wisdom. As an executive assistant, she used her talent and creative abilities to support colleagues and contribute to their success in business. Her challenges have included two near-death experiences, losing her mother very young, and being the primary caregiver for her grandmother at a time when she was divorced and raising her son alone. She has learned from many diverse and amazing people during her journey.

Now retired, this grandmother loves writing, cooking, gardening, and sharing quality time with friends and family, especially her two granddaughters. Just when Judy was learning to accept life without a partner, God blessed her with an extraordinary husband who had lived in a prisoner-of-war camp as a child, a man blessed with the divine gift of seeing and communicating telepathically with souls that had crossed over. He added an entirely new dimension to her spiritual enlightenment. Widowed now, Judy White-Artz lives in Plano, Texas.

My Journal

Intentions, Gratitude, Thoughts, and Reflections

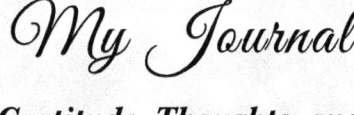

My Journal
Intentions, Gratitude, Thoughts, and Reflections

My Journal

Intentions, Gratitude, Thoughts, and Reflections

My Journal

Intentions, Gratitude, Thoughts, and Reflections

My Journal

Intentions, Gratitude, Thoughts, and Reflections

My Journal

Intentions, Gratitude, Thoughts, and Reflections

My Journal

Intentions, Gratitude, Thoughts, and Reflections

My Journal

Intentions, Gratitude, Thoughts, and Reflections

My Journal
Intentions, Gratitude, Thoughts, and Reflections

My Journal

Intentions, Gratitude, Thoughts, and Reflections

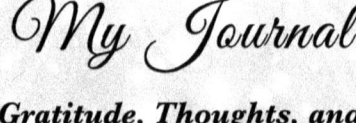

My Journal

Intentions, Gratitude, Thoughts, and Reflections

My Journal

Intentions, Gratitude, Thoughts, and Reflections

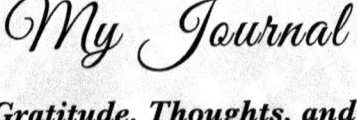

Intentions, Gratitude, Thoughts, and Reflections

My Journal

Intentions, Gratitude, Thoughts, and Reflections

Fresh Ink Group
Independent Multi-media Publisher
Fresh Ink Group / Push Pull Press
Voice of Indie / GeezWriter

Hardcovers
Softcovers
All Ebook Formats
Audiobooks
Podcasts
Worldwide Distribution

Indie Author Services
Book Development, Editing, Proofing
Graphic/Cover Design
Video/Trailer Production
Website Creation
Social Media Marketing
Writing Contests
Writers' Blogs

Authors
Editors
Artists
Experts
Professionals

FreshInkGroup.com
info@FreshInkGroup.com
Twitter: @FreshInkGroup
Facebook.com/FreshInkGroup
LinkedIn: Fresh Ink Group

Inspiring and unforgettable, Letting Go into Perfect Love is a riveting account of a journey through the terror of domestic violence to a faith that transforms all. As a college administrator, Gwendolyn M. Plano lived her professional life in a highly visible and accountable space—but as a wife and mother, behind closed doors, she and her family experienced unpredictable threat. Every nine seconds in the United States, a woman is assaulted or beaten—but to Gwen, this was her secret; it was her shame. Alternately heart-wrenching and joyful, this is a story of triumph over adversity—one woman's uplifting account of learning how to forgive the unforgiveable, recover her sense of self, bring healing into her family, and honor the journey home. Accompanied by glimpses of celestial beings, Gwen charts a path through sorrow to joy—and ultimately, writes of the one perfect love we all seek. Gwen's story is heartbreakingly familiar. It provides insight into the phenomenon of domestic violence. Understanding that murky world may provide the reader with the skills to help his or her sister or friend or even neighbor. Whether victim or friend, readers will be inspired by the author's courage.

Hardcover • Paperback, Ebooks • Audiobook

www.ingramcontent.com/pod-product-compliance
Lightning Source LLC
Chambersburg PA
CBHW070540170426
43200CB00011B/2490